RUNES

RUNES

EXPERIENCE AND GNOSIS OF A MODERN RUNE WALKER

Kenn Edwards, Rune Walker

Kenn Edwards

First Printing, 2023

ISBN (paperback) 979-8-9887782-3-3
ISBN (ebook) 979-8-9887782-5-7

www.runewalker.com

Kenn Edwards
PO Box 188
Stockton, Utah
84071
USA

Dedication

To name one requires me to name all. And that is impossible without my mind forgetting someone. Thank you to all of those who have supported, inspired, and challenged me in the creation of this work and in my life.

Thank you to the Runes, Gods, Giants, other beings, and Ancestors of the Traditions of pre-Christian Northern Europe for their influence on my life and work.

I dedicate this work to the Runes.

Contents

Introduction

Like most first-time print authors, writing this book has taken me several years. There are many obstacles to writing a book. I have faced many of them.

I have attended many online webinars and read many articles to prepare me to write and self-publish. Inevitably in every educational presentation, there comes a time to discuss the WIIFM, What's In It For Me. From here, it's all about planning the harvest of this labor, and there is always a dollar sign attached to it. This is then based on how well we can attract people to the book and how well we can distribute it. From my days as a corporate consultant, I understand all of these ideas and processes. It is beneficial and can be lucrative. I have been caught up in this process, impeding the progress. I would not change it, though.

This book is not part of a strategic plan to catapult me to the top of the best-seller list and get me more clients, translating to more money. It can not be. The parameters outlined by the aforementioned presentations make it impossible to write the book without considering its appeal to the consumers and, ultimately, the profit. The Runes can be and have been, brutally honest about many things in my life, and this book is no different. Write without thought of any of that. Write what you know because you've experienced it.

Having a background in education and training, I think of the reader and how best to facilitate their absorption and application of the material. Again, this structure has its own set of confining rules. My experiences with the Runes have been anything but limiting. My writing approach to the book must align. My WIIFM must align. My fulfillment comes from finishing the damn thing and publishing it. Having it available for those seeking information and a connection to the Runes is secondary.

Although there is a price to purchasing the book, my fulfillment is not in the profit. Of course, compensation is necessary and can neither be skipped nor ignored; one of the beautiful pearls of wisdom from Gebo, a Rune of gift, exchange, and balance.

This book is full of my experiences and kennings as the Runes manifest themselves in my life and the lives of those I teach, counsel, and partner with. Rune Walking in Modern Times is just that, walking forward into the horizon with the Runes and their wisdom. This requires me to bring up something else that needs to be addressed.

I created the title Rune Walker as a container to hold all the different aspects of my work. I am a psychic, healer, teacher, mentor, and medium, and the list goes on and continues to grow as I grow. It would be disrespectful of me to leave out the fact that I can and do receive knowledge from the Runes, gods, and ancestors, not only from the Rune poems and modern Rune workers/writers. Our ancestors respected and honored both the wisdom of the seen and unseen.

When I first began my relationship with the Runes, I struggled to bridge the gap and see their wisdom as relevant to my life. This was my primary reason for beginning to teach classes and writing this book many years ago.

My words I now add to the collective voice of those from the past and those from the present. I add my experiences and stories to enrich the tapestry and bring the threads of the Runes and old ways of my ancestors into our current conversations. I search for ways to connect, with honor, the place I live now to those European lands far away and the ways of my ancestors to my life as a descendent of settlers in a home far from my ancestral hearth. I am not the only one. May the stories of my journeys with the Runes inform and inspire.

Join me as our paths converge for a little while as we explore the wisdom of the Runes.

> **Hearth** is one of my most loved concepts. Hearth is the area in front of a fireplace. Hearth is where we cook, warm ourselves, and share stories. Hearth is imperative. Where is your hearth?

My Hearth & Viewpoint

Knowing some things that influence my perspective is helpful. It is unnecessary to agree with them all. We can share our perspectives and experiences without fear or threat. You can take what you need and leave the rest.

This book may not be considered an introductory text. I say this primarily because the Runes are part of a bigger picture. Their context is that of Northern Europe's Norse and Anglo-Saxon peoples and beyond. Therefore, I will reference those deities, stories, and other ideas. I will do my best to provide explanations. I encourage you to do your own research. Please do not let this prohibit you from readings further. There is much wisdom to be found in the Runes.

> **Wyrd** is similar to the concept of fate. Wyrd is what must be. I see it as a great tapestry on a loom. The pattern that emerges based upon the repetition of our actions. Some may propose that it is out of our hands. The Nornir ensure that the results of our actions are inescapable, unlike how we use the term Karma today.

At the forefront of my worldview sits a concept exemplified by the Nornir. The Nornir are three giantesses who sit at Urd's well in the World Tree's roots. The Nornir are responsible for ordering the Wyrd. They keep the past, present, and future in order. Their names can be interpreted as "that which is", "that which is becoming," and "that which must be." To paraphrase the words of an irreverent wise woman, Ingrid Kincaid: You can't harvest barley if you plant corn. This idea is a cornerstone in my life. How many times do we do the same things over and over again, expecting a new outcome? We must take responsibility for our actions and results. This is key.

I am a contemporary Heathen. I use the word Heathen only because it describes people of the heath; the people from the wild land, uncultivated. I do not try to reconstruct life as it was or believe that the cultures from which the Runes came are better than my current culture. We need to accept the current climate (social, political, and cultural). This acceptance does not mean we can not fight to change it. In fact, we should fight to change it. The Runes can give essential keys to finding ourselves and contentment. They also provide vital ideas for living in a balanced relationship with others in our communities.

> **Heath** is an open, uncultivated land area with characteristic heather, gorse, and coarse grasses vegetation, especially in Britain.

In my tradition, there are nine worlds held together by the World Tree. Deities in other cosmologies exist as well. The practices of my ancestors were passed by breath, not the written word. Because of this, much has been lost. Are we able to retrieve what was lost? We can. What I believe to be more important is that we reconnect with these deities and beings now. They have grown and changed over the millennia just as humanity has. I believe in unverifiable personal gnosis (UPG). I and many others have received communication from and continue building relationships with the Old Gods, our Ancestors, and the Runes. How do you think the information was obtained in the first place?

We should encounter and study the Runes in the order that They are willing to come forward and work with us. Therefore, when it comes time to read about each Rune, I want you to look at Their shapes and start with the Rune you feel pulled to. The one that seems to stir an emotion in you. You will be surprised at how appropriate and applicable the wisdom is in your life at that very moment. The Runes are best lived and remembered, not memorized.

Remember is an idea I use often. The wisdom of the Runes resides within us. Much like trying to remember a name or number we have learned, we can remember the Runes.

Predator & Prey

Let me get straight to the point. Humans are not at the top of the food chain. We can get fucked up by things in this physical world and the unseen otherworlds that are bigger and stronger.

I have worked with hundreds of clients, and we must cultivate significant spiritual development, boundaries, and protection skills. One of the first building blocks is understanding that we can set and hold boundaries. The key to this is comprehending the idea that you have the power to do this.

I often see this when clients express that they are constantly bothered by spirits or energies, making it difficult for them to function within their normal parameters. Unfortunately, they usually tell me this through tears because it has happened for so long. When I state that they have control over this, their expressions begin with disbelief and end with curiosity. It is a process of deconstructing old belief systems and patterns to build a new way of interacting with the seen and unseen worlds. This is where the Runes come into the picture. Their wisdom is transformational and practical.

In this book, you will read about my experiences with the Runes. I have cultivated my relationships and practice over nearly two decades and continue to do so daily. When you invite or ask the Runes to come into your life, They will work in Their own ways. They are individual and complete beings with Their own natures.

You can ask Them to work in certain ways, but this does not mean They will always comply.

For instance, several years ago, I asked Thurisaz, Rune of chaos, destruction, and deconstruction, to come into my life. It was almost a year of complete collapse. But I had only asked it to help with a few small things. Thurisaz can be uncontrollable and insatiable. I realized that much of what collapsed and fell to the wayside hindered me. There have been very few times, if any, where the Runes' interactions were not helpful in ways I could only realize once the chaos had concluded.

If you wish to develop relationships with the Runes, you must be willing to dedicate time to them. You will need to establish a personal development/spiritual practice. This entails an approach and discipline in which you can stand sovereign in the center of your life and bring all you are to the relationship and interaction. I invite you to read the book and research other writings and teachings before committing to a long-term relationship with the Runes. Wisdom can be found here, no matter your path or worldview.

I am including a few short sections about centering, grounding and shielding at the end of the book. These are foundational to any spiritual development or practice. If you intend to court the Runes, these or similar are necessary.

Endarkenment

To be perfectly upfront with you about this term, I got sick of the term "enlightenment." It had connotations of being somewhere to get to, a destination outside our current bodies. So, I changed it up.

I define endarkenment as turning knowledge into wisdom by finding where it resides/resonates in your body.

Our bodies are the tools with which we interact with the seen and unseen worlds. Through my UPG, we have three major Centers of Knowing: Intellect, Emotion, and Instinct. They are located in the head, lower chest, and lower abdomen. The positioning may vary slightly. Generally, we consider the brain the only place to process information and input; however, our other Centers of Knowing can also process information.

Knowledge can be seen as the energy of a thought that comes into our Intellect. Endarkenment is moving this energy/thought into the other two Centers of Knowing. Allowing the Emotion and Instinct centers to process the energy or thought enables the body to remember the wisdom it already carries. The result of this process usually involves a feeling or sensation in the body where the wisdom is stored.

In my experience, the Runes' wisdom can be very visceral. Set aside some time to sit with your different Centers of Knowing.

Focus on one Center of Knowing at a time. Keep the sessions separate. Create the intention of connecting to and communicating with each. Once connected, ask the following questions and record your answers in your journal or similar.

Before you begin, I must interject a couple of good tips:

1. Before doing any deep emotional work on yourself, it is good to have a therapist or counselor arranged to assist you in coping with any complicated feelings or memories that may surface.
2. If you begin to be overwhelmed, remember that you can ground that energy. Allow it to go free so that you can continue to work.
3. If you become overwhelmed, do math or any other activity, such as a puzzle that engages your brain. It will shift focus and help calm you.

Question One: What is the sensation from this Center of Knowing that indicates a "yes" or an affirmation?

Question Two: What is the sensation from this Center of Knowing that indicates a "no?"

Starting with these two questions and becoming proficient in understanding the "yes" and "no" is extremely helpful in making decisions and becoming aware of those parts of our lives that are out of integrity and alignment.

Endarkenment and exercises like these are not merely two pages in a book, nor should this connection to your body be underestimated. Make time to get to know your body and how it communicates with you.

The End Becomes The Beginning

After finishing the last draft of this book and before having an editor work on it, I wanted to consult the Runes to see if there was something They thought I needed to add to the book. With this intention, I reached into my bag of wooden pieces. Four Runes in my hand held the answer. I was not surprised, although I did expect more of a yes-or-no-style answer.

The Runes that inspired the following prose do not need to be shown at this stage of your experience. I know you will find them on your journey.

It is necessary to find common ground upon which we can build relationships. We often expect the Runes (and otherworldly beings) to come when we call. No matter how great your mommy said you were, you will never get anywhere dictating to others (seen or unseen) what they should do. That was not necessarily included in the ideas from the Runes, but it is true. The wisdom in the following prose has been provided to help find common ground. Find the common ground!

"ONE"

Whispers roll past the skin
Ever so lightly and almost imperceptibly
Kissing the stray hairs of the child
Who has become grown
The last whisper
Before
The last exhale
Forced by the weight of the
Rich dark earth collapsing the body
Beginning the compression that allows
The expansion

Whispers roll past the skin
Heavy and forced like the geyser relieving itself
Another compression simultaneously
A contraction and a thrust
An explosion that alters all
The ripples felt for hundreds of years
The ripples felt in the quivering muscles
The ripples emblazoned upon the grass beneath
Starting a fire of consumption
Consumption ending in Consummation

Whispers roll past the skin
Cupped by little hands
Silence
Then a scream, shrill and high
One to wake the dead
Laughter and rumbling of bare feet
Thunderous like a spooked herd of cattle
Without the danger
Coupled hands whipped by the reeds of grass
As freedom explodes
Like a warm spring gust headed for the mountains

Whispers roll past the skin
Breath weaving the flowing fabric of us
Coupled hands caressed by the handspun,
Homespun threads from two fields
From two looms
From one well
Threads crossing one another
Like the arms and legs of
Two becoming one
Promises of care
Promises of work
Promises of Joy and Pain

Whispers roll past the skin
Hailing a new dawn
From the comfort of the one
The one that rises before dawn
Each dawn
Over and over
Blistered hands the colors of sunrise
Golden wheat cradled like a baby
Blistered and bleeding hands paint the sunset
Art made from need
Harvests of blood
For
Harvests of food
If we master the dance of seed and soil

Whispers roll past the skin
Ever so lightly and almost imperceptibly
Kissing the stray hairs of the child
Who has become grown
The last whisper
Before
The last exhale
Forced by the weight of the
Rich dark earth collapsing the body
Beginning the compression that allows
The expansion

"TWO"

1,000 miles per hour
That is approximately how fast the Earth is spinning
That means we are never motionless

Be Quiet
Be Still
Sit Still
Be Calm
Sit Cross-legged
Breathe
Quiet your mind
Quiet your body
Slow your breath

If the earth were to stop spinning
The atmosphere, at 1,000 miles per hour,
Would wipe out everything, like a chalkboard eraser

After hours of sitting
Or Trying
After hours of thinking
About Not Thinking
After hours of breathing
To Someone Else's Rhythm
After hours of solitude
But Never Finding Solace
After years of protections
Only To Be Imprisoned
After all of this and much more
Still No Stillness

Quiet
Absence of noise
Abstention from speech
Absence of disturbance
Tranquility

Might it be said that the disturbance is...
Hours of sitting
Or Trying
Hours of thinking
About Not Thinking
Hours of breathing
To Someone Else's Rhythm
Hours of solitude
But Never Finding Solace
Years of protections
Only To Be Imprisoned

Quiet
Absence of noise
Abstention from speech
Absence of disturbance
Tranquility
All come not from
Stillness
But from
Alignment

"THREE"

Blood
Is
Required

Bloodshed is not the End
Blood shed is not the Beginning

You can not put the payment on a credit card
You can not make monthly payments
The price must be paid
Before you take possession

Blood red leaves
Fall to the ground
Blood
Falls to the Ground
The Ground devours
The Ground
The Soup Pot
The Cauldron
The Womb

When asking for Change
You do not get change back
It is all or nothing

Mastery
Requires not only
Interaction and
Execution
It Requires
Execution and
Integration
It Requires
Knowing
Not just
Knowing How

Isolation is Vanity

"FOUR"

Innovation
Adventure
Life
Freedom
The Folk benefit from them all
The Folk may not value them all

If you are reading this
You are being called
You are being called to
The Horizon
You are being called to
Walk away from the
Safety
Comfort
Warmth
Provided by your folk

If you are reading this
You are being called
You are being called to
Ride
You are being called to
Mount the steed
Gallop
Trot
Meander
Wherever your body pulls you

If you are reading this
You are being called
You are being called to
The Ocean
You are being called to
Life
Rhythm
Flow
Abundance
Provided by the Mothers of Night and Deep

If you are reading this
You are being called
You are being called to
The Forest
You are being called to
Connection
Sound
Color
Aroma
Provided by Web and Wing
Provided by Hoof and Horn
Provided by Hole and Horn

If you are reading this
Know One Thing
You will be called
You will be called
Home
You will be called to
Recount your Adventures
You will be called to
Instruct
Advise
Cultivate
Providing new ways to your folk

Innovation
Adventure
Life
Freedom
The Folk benefit from them all
The Folk may not value them all

If you are reading this
You are being called
You are being called because
You Hear the Call
You Feel the Call
The Call to the Beyond

You Are The Horizon
You Are The Steed
You Are The Ocean
You Are The Forest
You Are The Call

The Runes

I feel the need to fuck things up here. I will begin with Gar, representing my connection and doorway to everything. After that, the order of the Runes in this book will be based on Their wishes. What does that mean? It means I pulled Runes from my soft black bag to create the order they appear in the book. Why? Because this is the first act of rebellion that allows Them to be free of the constructs humans have placed upon Them.

Furthermore, if you do as I suggest and read the book based upon which Runes call you, it doesn't matter anyway. And you are part of the fuckery!

The Runes are typically categorized into the Elder Futhark, Younger Futhark, and Anglo-Saxon Futhorc, although there are more. Their meanings have evolved over time and within the context of the communities that held them. In certain instances, Their shapes have also changed.

In this book, I provide the name and shape(s) that I use for each. However, I do use alternates occasionally and have included those. Numerous books on the origins and ideas concerning their usage and meanings exist. Those books are part of the conversations being had by people worldwide trying to make sense of our fascination and connection to the Runes and "ways" of the peoples of Northern Europe, our ancestors.

We are missing the essential "hearth fire" that gives a center from which we can view and interact with the world. This book is one way I can connect and contribute to the conversation. A conversation that I hope supports our living, breathing, and evolving relationships with the Gods, Spirits, Runes, Ancestors, and Ways of the peoples of pre-Christian Northern Europe and people everywhere.

May you find memories in my stories, experiences, and poetry. May you find your hearth. May the relationships you begin to foster here lead to fulfillment and wholeness.

> **Redefine Boundaries**, remove the binary construct from the Runes, and see their characteristics and meanings as existing on a spectrum rather than only polarizing concepts such as good and evil, light and dark.

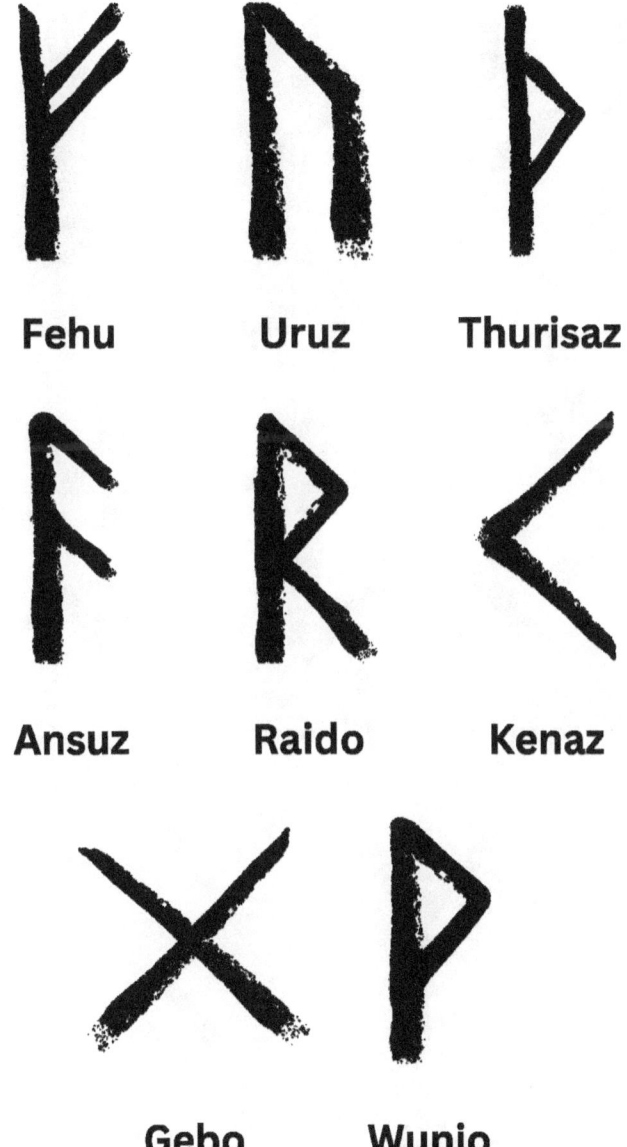

Fehu **Uruz** **Thurisaz**

Ansuz **Raido** **Kenaz**

Gebo **Wunjo**

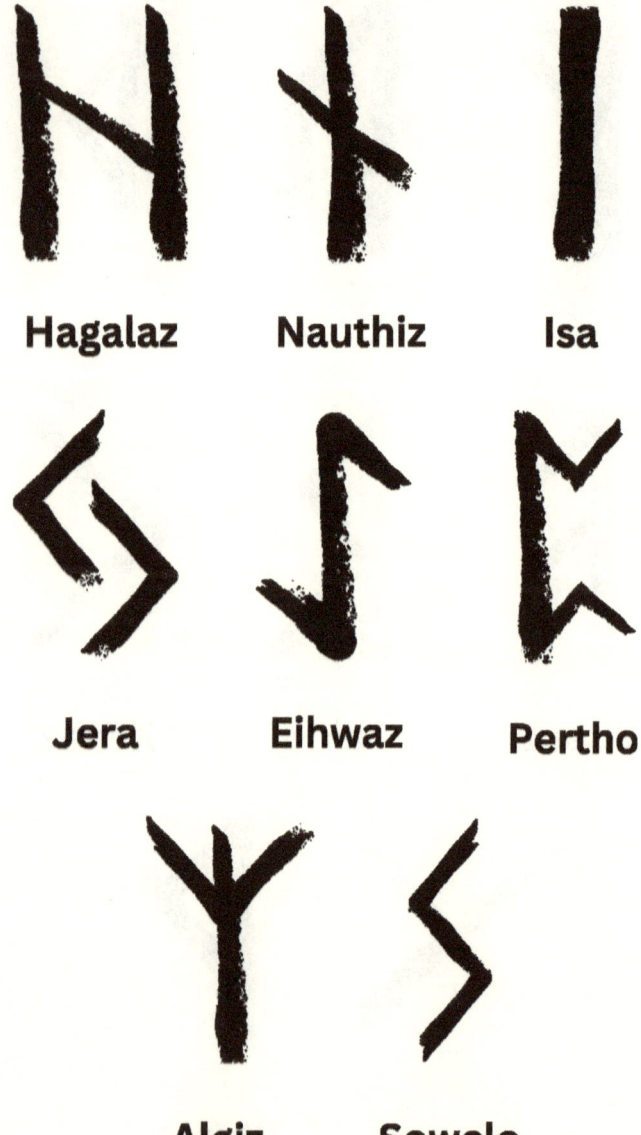

Hagalaz   **Nauthiz**   **Isa**

Jera   **Eihwaz**   **Pertho**

Algiz   **Sowelo**

Teiwaz **Berkana** **Ehwaz**

Mannaz **Laguz** **Inguz**

Othila **Dagaz**

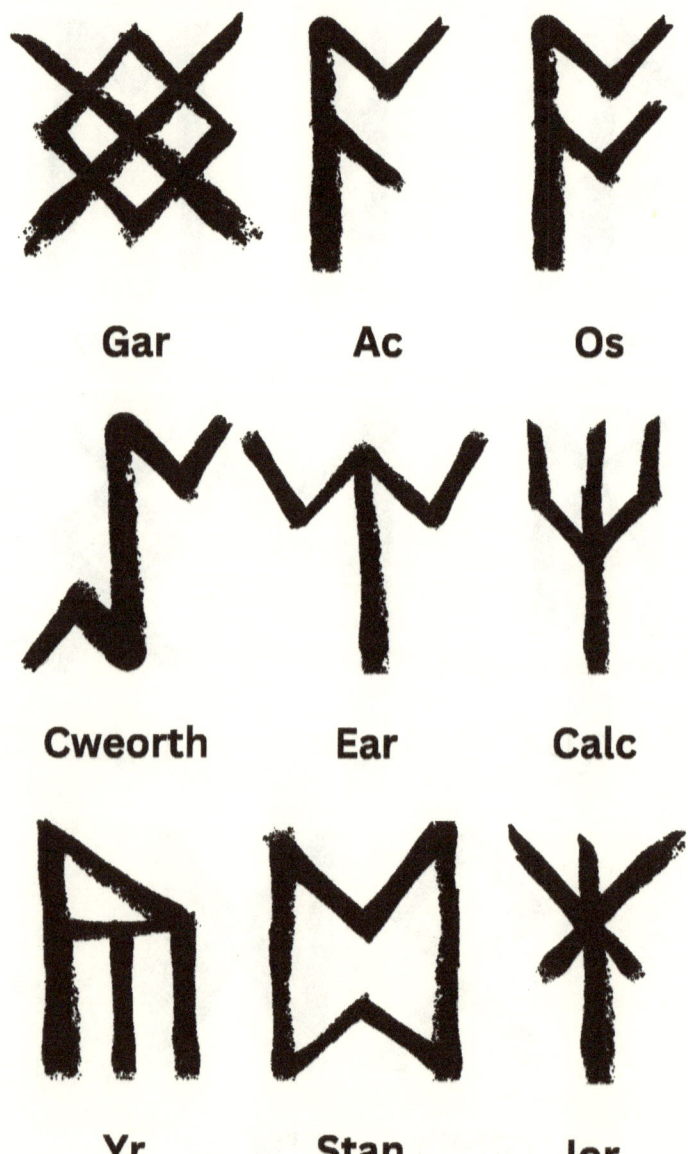

Gar **Ac** **Os**

Cweorth **Ear** **Calc**

Yr **Stan** **Ior**

Gar

Themes & Stories: Not To Be Known, Connection, Sacrifice, Initiation, Odinn, Yggdrasil (World Tree), Odinn's Spear
Deity: Odinn, Yggdrasil

Gar

Stop
But Not to Me
Connection to The Tree

The Green Glow
Holding
All Nine Worlds

The Spear
Shows Blood
Sacrificed to Surf
The Green Waves

The Inguz
Pierced by
The Gift

The Sacrifice
Required
To Pass

Gar

I have two beautiful goddaughters and a godson. The oldest is two and a half years old and talks up a storm. One day I was babysitting. She and I had fun making videos of her screaming and giggling on my phone. She is a giant ham when the camera comes out. She constantly wants my jewelry to put on and keep. Learning what ownership is at that age must be frustrating. I was showing the videos to my family and friends, and that's when I noticed something that stopped me in my tracks.

On this sunny afternoon, she pointed at a necklace I had made. It is fabricated from clay and marked on both sides with symbols. At first glance, it has an overall medium brown tint, but then the colors begin to pop out: green, yellow, and purple. And then, the silvery glaze shows itself as the talisman is shifted and turned in the light. The one side (I see it as the back) has a symbol consisting of two Runes, Kenaz and Raido. I use this as my Rune Walker signature, so to speak. The other side has Gar carved into the clay. One could say, it has two Runes as well. Gar does look like Gebo and Inguz laid together, or even two Inguz or four Gebo. My goddaughter looked at that necklace and said, "Look at this door."

I'm glad I recorded this because I had to listen to it again. I guess I didn't think much of it when it happened initially. She called it a door. She was right. Gar is my door, my gateway to the World Tree, Yggdrasil, and everything connected.

My Gar Pendant

A few years ago, I was journeying, spiritually or astrally, with a friend of mine, Chris. His wife, an extraordinary psychic medium, Kelli, sat in the room to help us "see" better if things became unclear.

When I open sacred space and my connection, I draw Gar and open the portal with a series of hand movements. Kelli was sitting behind her husband, out of my view. I leaned forward and opened the portal. I leaned back into my chair to settle in. "A big wooden door with Runes just appeared, and you guys need to go through," she said. I opened my eyes sharply to see they both had their eyes closed. I was stunned that she saw what I do on an energetic level. Wholly unique and validating.

When we are taught what Gar means, we are often given the "Stop asking. You're not meant to know" response. I've only encountered that three times. Fairly recently, Gar showed up in the Rune casting when working with a client. I felt compelled to stop and convey the "You're not meant to know" message. Because this was a situation I had only encountered a few times, I really wanted to know the answer to the question. I reached down to look at the Runes and was struck with a stabbing pain in my abdomen. I promptly stopped looking and adjusted course away from that. The discomfort went away. What is that saying about curiosity and the cat?

"Why does Gar's meaning differ for this, asshole?" you're pondering. That is a good and valid question. Without assuming all of our ideas about ownership, it is Odinn's Rune, and those who find themselves in his camp may develop different relationships with Gar. In this day and age, where everything has to be fair and equal, this may seem unfair and unequal. It is. Fair and equal are very human concepts we try to impose on all things natural. The closest word we have would be balanced, maybe, and even that doesn't provide a picture we humans can understand. We believe we are at the top of the food chain, and we are not.

Why do I have different meanings for Gar? Ask Gar. Ask Odinn. Ask the Nornir. I know what I know and what I feel. It's not just this way with Gar, mind you. All of the Runes choose for themselves what parts to show and offer. You and I do the same thing daily with people we meet. Just because we dial the phone number to reach Fehu doesn't mean the call will be answered or we will hear back when we leave a message after the beep.

As I sit here opening myself to Gar, I ask, "What do you want me to share, Gar? What part of you is meant to be shared in this exploration of the Runes?"

Let's remove the idea that the personality traits of Gar must be applicable in Rune casting/readings. The different facets of Gar and all of the Runes are like brilliant black diamonds spinning in the green light of Yggdrasil, providing countless glimmers, reflections, and depth.

I see connectedness, the grand tapestry, the great web. There is movement into a place of being able to traverse the bridges and pathways connecting the Nine Worlds. Gar is the sacrifice of the self. One's own participation in their own sacrifice. Hold the spear or knife to one's own throat and cut it, not because we want to die but because that is the sacrifice required to gain the wisdom, to become initiated. To become you.

On a more mundane level, I have seen Gar as the lack of movement into another space/initiation. I see it as holding on so tightly because we fear what is on the other side.

The sigil representing Gar can be seen as a few Runes and/or combinations. Where does it take us as it is unlocked and opened with each combination? Does it connect us with our Gods? Does it connect us with our unencumbered selves? Does it take you back to the beginning when darkness was light, and Gar was the green glow of Yggdrasil?

Mannaz

Themes & Stories: Contracts/Agreements/Boundaries Between People, Community, Handfasting, Building Community

Agreed

Blessed

as long as
You Uphold
Your End of
The
Contract

as long as
They Uphold
Their End of
The
Contract

Social
Contracts
Partnerships
Marriages
Lovers
Friends
Community
Held Together
by
The
Promises
Kept

Inevitably, many clients will want to ask about a relationship during our time together. Not just romantic, although those are popular subjects, but family and work relationships as well. I see Mannaz as the balance, agreements, and boundaries within relationships. I see Mannaz as two Wunjo Runes facing each other. I experience these Wunjos as two complete and whole beings coming together to form a third being, not coming together to complete each other. I also see it as two Isa runes holding a Gebo, which speaks to the balance of exchange necessary between two people or entities.

Mannaz can signify the balance, or lack thereof, in relationships. Many things can cause these imbalances. Sometimes those are clarified with other Runes or can be through psychic forms of communication as well. Beyond the reasons for the imbalance is this little golden nugget that is essential in Mannaz: We must keep up with our contracts through fulfillment and renegotiation. This becomes an "ah-ha" moment for married clients facing challenges. The moment they realize they have been operating under the same contract made on their wedding day while everything has changed, including their wants and needs, is a breakthrough.

In the chapter about Gebo, I state that balance is not static, and I feel the same here. Our marital and social contracts and boundaries are constantly ebbing and flowing because we are as well. We are each changing and growing. There is need for renegotiation.

I have also experienced Mannaz as the image of one looking in the mirror. This has been a rare experience but a valid one. In the concept of balanced relationships, Mannaz was there to illustrate that the client was not showing up for themselves. In other words, there was no self-care. Another aspect is that we are not separate from the unseen, meaning deity, divine, or even our energetic body. In this case, we can look to Mannaz for assistance aligning our lich (physical body) and hame (energy body).

Mannaz is a very appropriate rune to represent marriage or handfasting. Therefore, it is one I incorporate when conducting these ceremonies. Mannaz is a Rune that speaks to the binding together of people and thus can represent community. I have experienced this as a lack of community for an individual. At the beginning of the book, I spoke about the Runes giving wisdom for how to live in this world. This is such an appropriate topic for our current (2023) lives. One thing we need is community. We lack a sense of belonging. The pure presence of Mannaz shows how important it is for us to have community and to be in a balanced relationship with other people. We need each other.

Ear

Themes & Stories: Death & Burial of the Dead, Decomposition, Disassembly, Slow Passage of Time
Deity: Hela

#1

One Day
Does Not Undo
17,171
Days
This Takes Time
Breaking It Down
To Base Elements
Death
Transition
Transformation

The Missing Link
Between
Us
&
The Dirt

#2

Death Is Not Vindictive
It Just Is
You Must
Pay The Price for Life
Pain Is Not The Price
Death Is The Price

Allowing Your Account
To Go into
Collections
Or
Filing
Bankruptcy
Are Not Options

As I sit here thumbing through my journals and notes, I see the entries of the person that I used to be. I see the moments of awe as my path unfolded with each step. I see the struggles. I see the hope that I would be where I am today. Today could not have happened without yesterday, and tomorrow can not be fully embraced without today's death. This concept applies to so many things.

Journal entry, 4 December 2013:

> "Hel's rune (I feel that strongly), the rune of the grave. The cycle of life and death, time to let go. The only thing I can control is my attitude."
>
> "What is coming is always the question that cannot be answered until it arrives."
>
> "Must be willingly offering it up."

This is an excellent place to talk about Hel or Hela. I have a strange fascination or remembrance of Hela. I feel drawn to Her for sure.

I always take my Runes and my staff and invite any ancestors, Gods, Runes, or other beings to be present and witness the tattoos being marked on my skin. The day I got the facial tattoo around my left eye was no different.

I knew it had significance beyond my current comprehension. I lay on the table, and just as the needle began to penetrate my skin, I heard, "Death Mask! Death Mask! Death Mask!" It repeated several more times. No one else heard it, and it somewhat startled me.

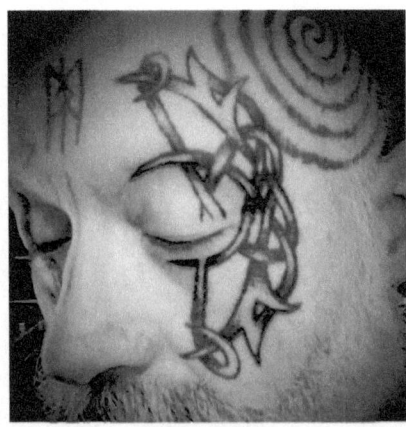

I've known for a long time that death walking is part of my journey. And I've known for a while that this particular tattoo was to be there. I didn't understand the significance or importance. The "Death Mask!" chanting was so intense that I opened my eyes to see if my friend/tattoo artist had heard it too. He didn't, but I did.

Hela is the daughter of Loki and Angrboda. She is a giantess. She is said to be half a beautiful woman and half a decomposing corpse. She has become vilified and left out in the cold because Christianity has done the same thing to death. Death is so feared that we continue to invent new technologies and products that keep us alive longer and looking youthful. To embrace her is to embrace the whole process and cycle we live. You must embrace the decomposition and rot as well as the soft and beautiful. To live balanced, we must accept the transition from this physical life into the next.

If Ear comes to you or you call to it, you must offer up something. If you don't, it will take what it feels is necessary. I imagine the image of the Reaper when I think of Ear in these terms.

One applicable instance I recall with Ear was during a reading for a client. It indicated that she and her husband's relationship had changed and shifted, but they were not letting go of it and embracing what it had become. If your hands are full holding the reins of the dead horse you're dragging, you can't use them to do anything else. You're stuck until you can let the reins go.

Other Runes can signify transitions and transformations. Cweorth is flash transformation, fire consuming instantly. Dagaz is transformation through the marked passage of the cycle, whether night into day or a seasonal passing of time. Because Ear is the Rune of the Grave, it can represent the slow transformation, one of slow decomposition and deconstruction. Slow isn't bad, as we've been taught in today's fast-paced world. I've even told myself, just let Cweorth take it in a flash, but that's the impatient me.

As a side note, I have experienced Ear in other Rune castings as an indicator that the client has had a literal death in the family. It has indicated miscarriages for clients as well. During readings, I allow the Runes to place images in my head corresponding to the meaning during this casting. I don't immediately go to literal physical death. By way of a more commonly known comparison, when someone gets the tower card in a tarot reading, they often immediately think the worst. But this is not always the case. The Runes, like tarot, have much more meaning than just the one-word descriptions we assign them.

A friend messaged me one Sunday afternoon and asked if I could judge a Cinco de Mayo karaoke contest that night. One of her judges had bailed. I thought, Hell yes. I would go to a local bar, hang out, have a few beers, and relax with friends.

I showed up at 8 p.m. as directed. The place was getting busy, but I didn't know anyone there except my friend, who was bartending. I chatted with her and the DJ, another friend of mine. It being Cinco de Mayo, I thought the karaoke competition must be for that. Little did I know that it was to raise money for the family of a deceased woman I was acquainted with. We were not friends, and she wouldn't even recognize me. When I fully comprehended the situation I was in, I could do nothing but shake my head. Of course, I would be offered this experience. This experience of seeing the grieving of a lost loved one who, as we would say, died too young. Of course, I would be there. I would be there to witness the deceased breeze through and watch her family and friends get up and sing for her, to her in many instances. It was not my place to channel messages or connect with the deceased. It was my place that night to watch this part of the death process and our interaction with it.

As a psychic who can connect with the dead, Ear is an important Rune to know. It is a connection to the dead and the realms of the deceased. Not having it would be like losing the phone number, email, and other contact information of someone you need to speak to.

One more association that I want to discuss is that of the singletree. A singletree can be used to hold up the carcass of a dead animal for butchering. This is a delicate procedure where the person, or butcher, separates the parts of the animal for use as food, leather, etc. It is important to note that when done well, everything is well-spent. All aspects are used. This can be a concept lost to us because of our throw-away society.

My final, pun intended, connection to make with Ear is represented by the burial process in which we are placed into a sealed box and lowered into the ground. This is another representation of our disconnection from the cycles of the living earth we are a part of, not separate. Our molecules and pieces do not go back into the ground to be broken down into components that feed the animals and plants that provide the next generations of people. Ear reminds us that when we die, we live on by reallocating our parts to sustain the cycle. It is dangerous for us to ignore this.

Today could not have happened without yesterday, and tomorrow can not be fully embraced without today's death. This concept applies to so many things.

Jera

Themes & Stories: Growing Cycles, Timing, Harvest, Intention

Deity: Jord, Nerthus

a year and a day

Cycle
Yes
Cycles
Yes

Reward
After
Hard Work
Yes
Knowing
When
IS
Key

Have you ever experienced times when no matter how hard you tried or pushed to get something going, it just wouldn't happen? We frequently wait to do things under the premise of waiting for the right time. Is it really why we're waiting, though? I would like everyone to be so in touch with their own personal creation cycles (I do not mean reproductive cycles) that we are waiting because we know we have a better chance of success if we wait.

I say it a lot, I'm sure, but Jera is one of my favorite wisdom-keepers when making shit happen. Jera teaches us that there is a harvest after a season of hard work and devotion. I am prone to having an idea that excites me but not always being able to follow through completely. This is where Jera comes in quite handy for me personally.

It is beneficial to get this Rune when someone asks about a project they are working on. More recently, though, I have had a string of readings where Jera has shown up to say, "Is it the right time to do this?" This is specially reinforced if Isa shows up in the casting. In our modern world of going to the store every time we need food, we forget the seasonality. I almost want to thank Star-bucks for not having Pumpkin Spice Lattes all year round. It's the closest thing we get to seeing seasonality.

Most of us forget that there must be a time when the ground lays fallow. This is a critical time in which soil fertility is restored. It goes without saying that if you plant in infertile soil, your crop, if it grows, will be weak. Jera's wisdom on this is priceless for us when it comes to our food production and also when it comes to our own cycles and projects.

In another aspect of the growing food cycle, Jera can be a good reminder that part of the harvesting process isn't just about con-suming. Part of the harvest is saved to use the seeds to plant next year's crop. One crop cycle is not isolated from the previous or the following. I hope you hear me when I say this isn't just about food production.

I love painting, watercolors specifically. I do painting in acrylics from time to time as well. The pattern I've noticed over the years is that I feel pulled to the paintbrushes during winter. I am most productive artistically during those months. When are you most creative? Do you try to force the art out of you before it's time? Would you birth a baby halfway through gestation because you wanted it to come out? That is another deep wisdom of Jera; You cannot plant the seed one day and harvest the next. This is a Rune of time and patience, not pushing. Things take time to form, my friends. Allow them to develop fully. Rushing it leaves you with little to no reward.

I'll leave you with this story. I recently conducted a reading for a young woman who had been attempting to connect to the Runes and other aspects of the Northern Traditions (Norse or Anglo-Saxon Paganism or Heathenry.) I stated that connecting with the seasons and cycle of the year was necessary. The response was illuminating. She said she could look up the seasons online, but what other way was there to connect with the coming spring? This response showed me how much we miss the basics of living on this planet. We have four distinct seasons locally. I am grateful for that. I told her to go outside. Begin noticing what trees were budding and which flowers and plants were beginning to break through the soil. It is not hard to know what part of the cycle we are in if we know the characteristics of and progression through the cycle.

Algiz

Themes & Stories: Protection, Fear, Imprisonment, Guarding Liminal Space

Arms Up to the Sky

Unseen
Wolves
surround
you
In The Forest
The
Protection
of
Your Making
that is
Now
Your Prison

Arms Up
Stand Up
Walk on

I stand in a forest clearing. It is a familiar place, the mountains of my youth. We hunted there. We hiked there. We collected firewood there. This visit is the product of a meditation where I slipped into a trance and journeyed away. The focus of my meditation was Algiz.

I stand in a forest clearing. Not a large clearing. Ferns opened up, seeming to catch the last rays of light as the sun passed below the tree tops heading for the night. This created many shadows in the forest. I began to sense Algiz in its defensive form. Forms.

Initially, I interpreted the tree line as the edge of my protective shielding. I reached out to it, but it wasn't a solid form or barrier. I felt it move through, just out of my reach. My logical Center of Knowing, my brain, took charge and tried desperately to make sense of the experience.

Because of the shape of the Rune, it may be an elk or moose moving just behind the tree line. That felt wrong. It moves closer to the ground. And feels hungry. I knew then it was a wolf or, rather, wolves.

This journey benefited me when learning how to set up wards and shields. I learned quickly that the more transparent I am about things, the better.

I was part owner of a metaphysical shop. We placed wards and shields around it to protect it from any destructive energy directed at us. I wanted this ward to allow the good stuff in and to allow people to see it for what it was so that they would not fear a pagan store in a predominantly Christian town. I designed the ward with many Algiz connected to look like a web. The destructive energy would be captured in the web, and the creative would go through.

To finish the journey story, I experienced something malicious coming at me from the forest. As it got closer, I wondered how this part of Algiz worked. I saw it get attacked and devoured by the wolves. The silent predator ambushed the thing before it even knew what was happening. This experience expanded my knowledge of the protective part of Algiz.

Another connected facet is that of the elk sedge. This is a plant that exists in wetlands and bogs. It is sharp. It can be seen as a protector of the liminal spaces. I've had my own experiences in bogs; they are liminal spaces between this world and the otherworlds.

When working with clients, I often experience Algiz as asking, "Where has your protection become your imprisonment?" This aspect was shared with me by Ingrid Kincaid. I use this simple story to explain this in client sessions. If a deer walks across a hillside of low brush and senses danger, it may lay down in the brush for cover and safety. If the deer never gets up and moves on, it will die there. Algiz points out and asks us to examine parts of our lives where we have done the same thing.

As a Rune of protection, Algiz can be incorporated into a fence design surrounding your property more practically and tangibly.

Ehwaz

Themes & Stories: Movement, Travel, Direction, Potential, Steady Progress, Workhorse

The Most Difficult Question

What
Do
You
Want

the Horse is Waiting

In Which Direction Will You Go
It's All Up To You

This can be one of the most straightforward Runes in the Nine Worlds. It is true in a very literal sense, not just figuratively. Ehwaz contains the power of moving forward, the power of movement. This is not a quick Rune, though.

When working with folks either in coaching or readings, the most challenging question for them to answer is this, "What do you want?' What do we want? Most of us know what we don't want. But this is not what Ehwaz asks.

A good visual representation of this concept is looking at the glyph itself. The focus of the glyph is the center point of the M. When I see it, I am reminded of a target or focal point. Ehwaz reminds us that energy is present for forward movement. We need to decide what to focus that energy on.

Ehwaz is the Rune of the workhorse. The workhorse is very useful in getting things done. When preparing for a class recently, I wanted to know how much more power a horse had than a human. If we utilize horsepower as our unit of measure, a horse has 15 times more power than a human. This made sense to me in terms of Ehwaz. The workhorse needs to be given a direction or goal, and it will put its energy into accomplishing it. It is far more powerful than we are. The potential energy is beneficial to us.

I mentioned earlier that it is not a quick Rune. Ehwaz is not valuable for delivering a message quickly, for example. There are several ways in modern times: email, text message, mailing a letter with overnight service, or regular old "it just needs to get there" mail. Ehwaz is very much the latter. Ehwaz signifies that you must walk every step of the way, and no shortcuts can be taken. There is so much wealth in walking every step of the way, even if it is over thorns. Too often in our modern time, we want things immediately and can get them directly. There is nothing wrong with that, per se. And there is so much to be gained by the experience of walking the path every step.

There is no right or wrong focus for Ehwaz. Remember, it is the power of movement. When little children have excess energy, we take them to the park or run around to get this energy out, primarily so we can focus and get things done. However, this happens to adults, as well. We can experience these energy surges and feel the need to recognize what they are or know what to do with them. For me, this surge of energy can sometimes create anxious feelings. I have worked with folks who have experienced this energy as being an energetic attack from an outside source. When this perception occurred, the client directed Ehwaz's energy into defending themselves. This can add to the problem when the energy is meant to move, not to be used to build a castle around us and hold us in one place. Another way to experience this is having one foot on the gas and one foot on the brake of an automobile.

Ehwaz can help us be conscious of where we choose to focus our energy. Where will you go with the energy of movement? How much richer will life be when you've walked every step?

Cweorth

Themes & Stories: Funeral Pyre, Rapid Transformation, Death, Release of Spirit
Deity: Surtr

Smoke Fills the Air
Rising High
from the
Neatly Arranged
Aspen Logs
Cradling The Dead

Flash
Crackle
Towering Inferno
Consumes All
Leaves
Shards of Bone
The Ash
Blows in the Wind
Rising High
to
Sail on the Winds
of
The Four Deer

One afternoon, I was working at the Blue Antler, a spiritual/ metaphysical store I co-owned. One of my students and a member of our small community stopped in. Their countenance was heavier than usual. They asked me if I could chat with them briefly about their experience with Cweorth. We stepped to the side, and the whole worrisome experience came rushing out like the water from a breaking dam.

The previous day they had completed a ritual in which they used Cweorth. The purpose of using Cweorth was to deliver the message/intent of the ceremony rapidly. I can understand the thought process: Cweorth is a rapid/flash transformation Rune. After the ritual, the candle used was allowed to burn out entirely. To be safe, the small candle was placed on a plate and left to sit inside the sacred circle that had been cast. The practitioner then shut the door to their ceremony room and went to bed.

The following day after waking up, they began to smell a faint burning scent. They searched the house looking at the heaters, toaster, oven, and anything that may put off that scent. After finding nothing, they realized it may have been the candle. They opened the door to their ceremony room. Fortunately, the room was filled only with smoke — there were no flames, only smoke. After opening the windows and clearing the smoke, they saw that the candle plate had broken in half. Furthermore, underneath the plate, a circle had been burned into the wood flooring that matched the bottom of the vessel.

They explained that although they had done this same ritual several times, without Cweorth, this had never happened. They were physically unsettled when telling me the story. It was the first time they had encountered the power the Runes truly could bring. Even though Cweorth represents the funeral pyre, a human concept, the power of fire is beyond our small conceptualization of natural and/ or primal. How would you feel if this happened to you?

I have had a few journeying experiences with Surtr. He is one of the most ancient of beings. He is the ruler of Muspellheim, the world of fire. He existed before Niflheim and Muspellheim collided. He is very, very old. Cweorth and Surtr are connected.

Sitting on the black sand beach at the edge of Muspellheim, I could glimpse the power of Surtr. The encounter was brief, yet I could sense the sacredness of this world of fire. The smoke and ash floated in the thick air. The feel of the black sand beneath me was unlike any sand I'd felt before.

Cweorth can bring a hallowing to something or somewhere. The consecration comes from the natural stripping down to bare elements and offering to sustain other life. In much the same way forest fires renew. In this way, I believe Cweorth can show us what in our lives needs to be burned to the ground and released so that new may come. Purification.

I must add this caution: Fire is not to be fucked with. We may still be burned even if we respect fire. Fire has an insatiable and uncontrollable hunger. It is powerful. Please be responsible.

I wish to be buried without the box or burned on a funeral pyre. Again, although it is the Rune of the Funeral Pyre, it doesn't always have to mean death. It is one beautiful embodiment of letting things go—more than letting them go, setting them on fire. Watching them whirl around a column of flames and whip up into the ether carried on the winds. This Rune signifies quick release and transformation. Sometimes things need to be buried, and sometimes they must be burned. My fellow shamans may pull Runes on how my body should be dealt with when I die. There is much wisdom in knowing or being able to find out which path you should take. Too often, when working with clients, I come across situations where they have buried things that should have been burned. Therefore, they are still dealing with the breakdown and undoing. Moving forward is hard when you're still waiting for the last thing to break down.

Cweorth also has ties to ancestral work or the ancestors. Most of us have experienced sitting around a fire telling stories or lying in front of a fire for a romantic evening. Our ancestors did the same. The ancestors of the Northern Traditions kept records through storytelling. I imagine this to be done around the warmth of the hearth fire. We can connect to this thread today.

Raido

Themes & Stories: Shamanic Journeys, Travel, Spiritual Movement, Sleipnir (Odinn's eight-legged horse)

I'm sure Eight Legs
sounds like a Thundering Stampede
set out across the Sky
set out across the across
to
9 Worlds
Captivated by the
First & Last
Breath of the Tree
In
&
Ex
hale
Rhyme Unknown
Reason Unknown
Rhythm Assured
Eight hooves
Pound out
the
First & Last
Breath
Taken
for a
Ride

I utilize a sigil to sign particular creative works of mine. Kenaz and Raido connected represent Kenn Rune Walker, Walker Between Worlds. This is where I will begin talking about Raido. It is a Rune of journeying.

Years ago, I attended a psychic fair-style event and read for a charming young woman. She had blonde hair and was, by all means, just a regular twenty-something adult. As most people, in my experience, she sat down with questions to ask but said she had none. We began with a general reading to see what was happening in her world. In combination with several other Runes, Raido lay on my lambskin before me. I interpreted the casting and asked her if this fits into her life anywhere, made sense, or shed light on her problems. She responded that it didn't. I scratched my head. I was reasonably sure I was on the right track. I kept asking questions, and we were going nowhere. I raised my hands and asked, "Are you going on a trip with a friend and want to take your car?" Her demeanor changed, and she sat up attentively and replied, "Yes!" I responded, "Don't go. Your car will break down. Take your friend's car."

This is a prime example of how the messages from and characteristics of the Runes can be both mundane and esoteric. That day, I learned a good lesson and now see that Raido isn't just about spiritual journeying. It can literally mean a trip or vacation.

I also associate the phrase "the journey is the destination" with this Rune. Ehwaz is another Rune associated with horses and, moving forward. The difference between the two is that Ehwaz is like a workhorse in the physical realm, and Raido is much more esoteric. Raido associated with the horse has much to do with its rhythm as it gallops or runs. The rhythm of the drum takes us into other worlds much the way shamans or similar would have used them in ancient and modern times. It is widespread to encounter workshops where one can make their own drum for personal practice.

With Raido having such a presence of forward motion, it is common to see its characteristics include spiritual ascent, finding and staying on one's path, and adding substance to one's wish or intentions. Raido and Ansuz may be a great help if you feel stuck.

Sowelo

Themes & Stories: Sun, Illumination, Enlightenment, Victory
Deity: Sunna, Thor

My Face
&
My Arms
Burnt Red
by my day
Communing
with
Sowelo

Wind & Road

What is your relationship
with the Sun

I've been
So
Inundated
with light
that I have
an
Aversion
to it

I'll stick
with
Illumination
in the
Darkest
Sense
of the word
&
with
Victory
as
Chosen
by the
Valkyries

I admit that I've had a challenge connecting with Sowelo. Maybe the better word is embracing or accepting some of Sowelo's wisdom. It is altogether possible that I have developed an aversion to "the light" — yes, the love and light mentality of modern New Age movements.

As I worked with Surt one day, I was shown the fire Runes together in one sigil. I was told to get that tattooed, and I did. Sowelo is the fire of the sun. Sowelo contains the power to provide light and warmth and to grow food. It also includes the ability to burn our skin and cause pain and suffering if we are too long in its rays. This is on a purely physical level.

My aversion to Sowelo comes from the less physical representations. Sowelo is victory. It is light. It is enlightening. It is comfort. It is positive. It is the Valkyries rising from the battlefield with the slain. Some of these aspects can be easily confused with things that we today may prefer to as "toxic positivity."

When I first began remembering the Runes, I became very upset with the amount of light and love that showered the spiritual community. I made fun of the "white lighters." I did so from a very pompous place with such limited vision. Sowelo helps me to accept that the positive and light things are part of life as well. It allows me to receive warmth from not just the sun but from others, from the community.

Sowelo carries the wisdom of the true balance of light. The Gods placed the sun in rhythms to provide a balanced system that would give life. The ever-turning wheel shows us that there truly is no light and no dark as independent entities. They come from the same source. It depends on our relation to it at any given moment.

I have also experienced Sowelo as a lightning strike. In this capacity, it can be a flash of inspiration. It also has shown itself to represent the sometimes tumultuous storm of someone who experiences what we may label as ADD or ADHD. These are, of course, meanings shown to me within specific contexts of client sessions. It is helpful to get to know them in more profound ways. The strike of "inspiration" is valuable and can be productive until we get multiple strikes that seem to interrupt each other, which can lead nowhere.

Ior

Themes & Stories: Liminal Space, Binary, Boundaries, Suppressed
Emotions/Memories, Serpent Energies, Subconscious
Deity: Jormungandr

My
First
Lover

You Who
Pierced
My Shields

You Who
Stirred
the Depths
of
My Ocean

You Who
Taught Me How
To Remember
My Body
My Connection
&
They Are One

You
Will
Always
Be
My First

Jormungandr, The World Serpent, is a snake or dragon living in the ocean surrounding Midgard, the visible world. The serpent is so giant that it completely encircles Midgard. Jormungandr is a sibling to Fenris, the great wolf, and Hel or Hela, who cares for Helheim, the realm of the dead. Jormungandr is the child of Loki and Angrboda. Jormungandr is connected to the Rune Ior.

Along with Kenaz, Ior is one of the Runes that first showed up to me when I began this journey. Before getting too far into this, Thor and Jormungandr are fated to battle at Ragnarok in Norse cosmology. Let's just briefly look at this interesting concept.

Thor is half-Aesir, a high god, and half-Jotun, or Giant. Thor represents overcoming the natural, maybe even what some would call the savage parts of ourselves that exist within and are not disconnected from the wheel of life on our planet. The high gods believed themselves to be more civilized than the Giants. This concept isn't new and is still applicable today. As I am writing this, just the other day, a friend of mine commented that I may be able to teach her daughter about photography, and her daughter responded with a comment that she already knew. Catching my drift?

If I can go further, I love that Jormungandr is a giant serpent. How fucking phallic is that? Thor battles his own sexuality, sexual drives, and desires. This happens in the final battle of Ragnarok. Let's leave Thor's cock alone for now. As I say that, I hear Him chuckle, and the thunder rumbles outside during this stormy spring season, literally.

I work with a lot of serpent or dragon energy. At first, this was a fanciful interpretation of the energies around me. Now, after years of experience, I know it to be true. I love to travel back in time using my journals to experience these new vantage point lessons that I learned back then. They're still absolutely applicable even now. A bonus of doing this is seeing the path and, hopefully, growth that I have experienced. Usually, we have such a limited perspective, and coupled with the fact that I can be impatient, it is helpful to see things from a bigger-picture view.

I mentioned before that Ior and Jormungandr came to me quite early in my journey back to my ancestral roots. At night I would sit at my altar and, by candlelight, gaze into the mirror. My vision would soften, and then I would journey. With the help of my journals, I go back there now and recollect several encounters that went something like this: A serpent that I concluded to be Jormungandr or Ior would present itself to me and ask that I swallow it (Now, get your minds out of the gutter ... or maybe not). Anyway, I said no the first time. I tried the few times that followed, but it always ended the same, with the serpent being rejected because I felt as if I were choking and unable to breathe.

I found in my journal the notes I had taken during a Rune reading with my friend Ingrid Kincaid. I had asked about this recurring event, and the reading stated that it was to combine my physical and spiritual bodies into one. However, at this time, I had to learn to walk in both worlds simultaneously. Later, I would learn that I am always in both and can be aware of both, not just one or the other.

Fuck, even I am a little confused trying to explain that. It's like this: Snakes do not travel in a straight line. If they move forward, they do so in an "s" shape. So, if there is a straight line and the snake moves along it in the same direction, its body is always on both sides of the line. I hope that makes sense. Having that imagery, we are constantly in the physical and spiritual worlds.

I accepted that I am in both worlds. A simple concept at first. The real energy is put into the next step: Where the fuck do I experience the Otherworld? I am receiving information from there, but where is that being stored? How do I access it? Big questions can be answered by working with Ior and Kenaz.

A few months later, the following journal account was recorded:

"Ior and Jormungandr visited me on my mound tonight. Jormungandr showed me that I need to be devoured by him so that as a bind rune, those things that bind me can be broken, and I can emerge from him to be free."

This prose is part of that entry:

I have been bound
held together by
crazy glue
stuck together
bound by my thoughts
thoughts birthed from a void
from a womb
from a concubine raped by a desert god
that I do not know
I share not his DNA
I share not her chains

I go now to the serpent and offer myself
to go deep inside its belly
to bathe in the bile
to burn away the glue that has bound me
It is the only way
I am grateful.

Ior can show you how to be on both sides of a situation and encircle the whole and not take sides. Ior can bring any self-imposed boundaries or boxes that need to be broken through to access your awareness. Jormungandr, with Their beautiful strength and tumultuousness, is a great ally when you need to break through those boundaries and expand your own world. I've always pictured riding on Jormungandr's back through the open ocean, finding the edge of the map, and busting past to see that there's so much more.

One great wisdom of this Rune is that it can help pull us out of the ideas of binary. Jormungandr is neither male nor female and is both. This shift in perspective allows us to experience the 99 shades of gray between black and white. The binary is a boundary that may have kept us safe at some point but inhibits our experiences of life with the seen and the unseen.

Thurisaz

Themes & Stories: Chaos, Destruction, Deconstruction, Raw Consumption
Deity: Fenrir, Thor, Loki

Green funnel crashes
To the earth
Whirling force
Jaws snap shut
Locked on prey
No fucks given
Either way
It just is
And
Must be
Must
Always
Be

This is not a Rune to be taken lightly. None of them are, actually. But this one, in particular, can be powerfully life-altering. It will wreck your life indiscriminately. I often use the words chaos, destruction, and deconstruction when discussing Thurisaz.

When I figuratively see Thurisaz in action, it is a tornado. It is raw. It is primal. It is potential in the moment of explosion. It is unbridled destruction. It is the essential part of the process that we often ignore or look down upon. We hate "endings." Who told you it was an ending? Maybe the moment of destruction/deconstruction is actually the beginning! Do you not need the pieces to build something new? Yes, I am an advertisement for destruction. I advocate for accepting and embracing that part of the process instead of fearing it. And it can suck going through it.

Several years ago, I made an amulet with Thurisaz inscribed on it. I then asked for Thurisaz to manifest in my life to help me. I was naive. I learned a lesson. That lesson lasted for a harsh six months. Every relationship I had was tested. Every project was touched somehow (and "touched" is putting it lightly).

Thurisaz is ravenous by nature. Whenever I began creating something new, it would get blown apart like a tornado had landed. It was more than frustrating until I realized that, in my case, my life needed to be taken apart and rebuilt. It was only when Thurisaz could no longer feed that it moved on. This rapidly repeating cycle of creation and destruction allowed me to recognize that I had been rebuilding my life using the previous blueprint that had not worked. If you put lipstick on a pig, it is still a pig.

I love the exhilaration of that fast-flowing energy and movement. There are results of that tornado touching down on top of your house. Would I do it again? Yes, but I'm a crazy bastard who likes changing things.

Have you ever lost yourself in the lustful passion of sex? I believe this is one way we get a glimpse of this power. But it's not just being horny. It's the moment when your breath is heavy and steady. The moment when you wrap your hand around your lover's throat and feel the throb of their blood racing through them. You squeeze gently and briefly, experiencing the ecstasy of consuming and taking their very life from them. Um, yeah, me neither.

This is not a Rune to approach with fear or trepidation. Thurisaz isn't there just to relieve your anger and help you feel better. I'm not even sure it can help you manage anger. I think the best it can do is help us look at this state of being and honor it, not reject or hate it. Honor the destruction that must and will always be the beginning of the end.

I experience this Rune as being connected to Fenrir, the wolf child of Angrboda and Loki. It can be connected to the Giants or Thurse and also Thor. In this way, it is very primal, raw, and natural. I see the same connections with Fenrir.

Dagaz

Themes & Stories: Passage of Time from one aspect into another, Dawn, Breakthrough

Time
Measured in Cycles
Passing
of
Passages
All
&
Nothing
to Be Something
to Go Somewhere
Crossing
Many Horizons
This
Measurement
is
Immeasurable
Infinite

Makes Me Fall
into
Liminal Space
Sleepy Mind
Turning Off

An overarching theme of transformation is often seen in Dagaz. It is the kind of transformation that happens as we become something and then nothing over and over again.

Years ago, I was reading for a friend and saw the Rune shape as the child's game Chutes and Ladders. I saw my friend begin at the bottom of one of the vertical lines of Dagaz, and as she climbed up, she gained skill in her career and became the best. When she reached the top of that vertical line, she descended across the middle, where she became nothing and started the process over. Of course, she did not "become nothing" but mastered what was placed before her and moved on to learning something else. Transformation.

During one incredibly esoteric-feeling class, I encountered Dagaz as I had never seen it before. Dagaz was the main focus of the discussion for that part of the class. We all sat on pillows around an altar of candles on the floor. The lights were low, and it felt like an ancient cave where we passed the lore over the roar of the old hearth fire.

I delivered the information written down in my class notebook. As always, I then asked Dagaz if it had any other wisdom that it wished to give. I closed my eyes. I saw Dagaz untwist. I had never imagined it would be twisted. The basic idea conveyed to me that night was this: Dagaz can be a way to bring two points in time and space together so we can move between them. It can be a portal. It can be used for journey work.

Dagaz can be seen as the dawn, any dawn — that heralds the breakthrough from the darkest part of the year to the lightest. Traditionally, daylight means gathering food, planting crops, and doing other things impossible during the long, dark winter. In this aspect, it can represent a time when we move into this very productive time.

Remember when I stated that the Runes are spectrums and not polarized opposites? On the spectrum of Dagaz, not only does it represent dawn, but it may also represent dusk. The idea that a day began with sunset is not out of place. I do not have all of the answers for you. This is a journey. And, it just so happens that my last stop on the Dagaz train was at this very idea. I am excited to explore this aspect. I hope you are feeling equally excited about your Rune journeys. Never stop asking questions and being exhilarated by life's potential.

Ac

Themes & Stories: Sovereignty, Endurance, Leadership, Oak Tree
Deity: Angrboda

To Earn Your Stripes
Is To Be
A Lightning Rod

Be Strong
Be Anchored

And
If Lightning Strikes
Be Explosive
And
Use That Fire

Much of what Ac represents can be gleaned from the story of Angrboda.

When I encounter Angrboda, it was usually in a training situation. The one constant is always that She carries her staff with her. This staff is her résumé. Everything you need to know about her is carved into this giant piece of oak.

Beginning at the very bottom, a sigil represents her first initiation. You'll need to do your own courting of her and ask her yourself to learn more about that. I merely see one red ring around the bottom of the staff that symbolizes that event. Rising up that beautifully sculpted oak piece from that ring are markings and colors, cloth and charms.

We must remember that the markings we may not recognize are from unsuccessful campaigns and/or the hundreds of hours of practice that went into preparing for them. Angrboda is a highly trained and accomplished warrior, leader, shaman, and mother. She is strong and sovereign. This is where the personality traits of Ac really show through for me.

Ac is connected to the Oak tree. Ac is strength. It is not brute force but the strength generated by years of growth. It is endurance. Mastery and individual strength are realized through accepting and embracing all one has experienced. This includes success and failures, love and heartbreak, public and private accolades, and persecution.

When Ac shows up in readings for clients, one of the powerful messages is to stand firm in your own power and sovereignty. Ac wants the querent to embrace the life they've lived and let that sustain and give the strength necessary to do what must be done.

I have also experienced Ac as a symbol that the person being read has just stepped into a leadership position of any kind. One clarification is that they have become this leader because their parent or head of their living family line has either died or become too weak to act as the leader. So in these terms, it's less like getting a promotion and more familial and ancestral.

Ac also challenges our beliefs about what we consider ugly, monstrous, and socially unacceptable. The Ironwood is full of beings that are very much unlike us in appearance. How will we react to one of these folks? Will we accept them? Hell, some humans still have a problem with other humans with different skin colors and who speak a foreign language. Ac's sovereignty also contains the ability to accept those around you regardless.

> **Ironwood** is a forest where Angrboda lives with other beings that would be considered unacceptable elsewhere.

Uruz

Themes & Stories: Aurochs, Strength, Wild, Untamed, Instinct

Wild
be Wild
Be
Untamed, free
Free yourself
Follow your Instincts
Your gut
Your blood
Line
Back all the way
Back
To the place and
Time
When we had
To
Had to
Trust
Our
Noses that told us
Of danger
Of food
Of sex

Trust
Your
Body
The recycled
Molecules
That make up
Your
Body
Have been around
Much longer
Than you
Respect that
Trust that
Trust them
And in so doing
You will
Find
You

Wild. Untamed. I love this Rune. I probably say that about every Rune, and I'm sure it's true at some point.

I will begin with a more modern facet of this Rune that I see in readings quite a bit. Uruz has appeared in readings to signify that the querent is far too domesticated in some areas of their life. Much like the European aurochs, we are in danger of becoming extinct. You may think I am being dramatic. However, have you ever reached that edge of breaking? You can't cry. You can't laugh. And yet there are tears. You can't move forward, and you find yourself literally or metaphorically huddled in a dark corner of your own. Our creativity and passion come from the wildness at our core.

Another example may be the wild mustangs. They are captivating and beautiful as they effortlessly cross the hills with rhythmic dust trails sailing into the sunset. When these horses are broken, their spirit becomes broken as well.

Uruz connects to the wild at the core of all beings. The untamed center is in tune with the rhythm of the cycle. The deer and elk living near me follow the seasons, moving north to south and up and down in elevation. This is the cycle we resist adopting a holiday calendar that keeps us busy during the coldest and darkest time of the cycle (in the northern hemisphere).

Uruz also led me to the concept of endarkenment. Remember, endarkenment is taking the knowledge one is given and allowing it to find, or not, its place in the body. Uruz is about the body's power and relationship with the wisdom held there. I believe the actual test of knowledge is if it can find its place in the body — where it already exists.

At times, I have also had Uruz represent an initiation. We have very few authentic initiations in modern life. This can mean a challenge, or challenging time, that will usher in a new worldview and way of being.

One final aspect I would like to discuss is Uruz has the ability to ground. Because it connects deeply with the cycles we live within, it can be partnered with to ground excess energies/emotions creating a stabilizing effect. In much the same way, it can also help us bring matters of the otherworlds into practical view and help them manifest in this physical existence.

Ansuz

Themes & Stories: Messages, Clearing, Wind/Air
Deity: Odinn

Like
Odinn
on the Winds
of the Terrible
Storm
It
Clears
&
Collects
The Land
Refurbished
The Forest
Anew
Collecting
Breath
the Breath
Our
Breath

More often than not, Ansuz shows up for me to indicate clearing of some kind. Like the clean-up after a tornado, Ansuz removes what is no longer needed or broken beyond repair or use.

I rarely teach the Runes in order, as you know. Looking at them in their order has benefits, and stories emerge. This is one of the occasions the Runes show the pathway and preparation to initiation or shamanic journey. In this instance, we can apply it to the first eight Runes or First Aett. The steps are straightforward and show us the path to initiation or how to journey to the otherworlds.

Fehu represents finding your worth and value. Uruz speaks to finding the unbridled self. Thurisaz is the destruction that must come before change can be made. Ansuz is the clearing away of any debris that will not be used. Raido then signifies the journey to the otherworld, and Kenaz the finding of the inner flame that guides oneself. Gebo is the requirement of an exchange or the deal made in the Otherworld for whatever we need. Finally, Wunjo represents the joy or madness of communing with the deities, possibly getting what you desire.

Ansuz feels much more like a calming breeze or a glassy flowing river. This is partly because there is a sense of renewal to it. It is as powerful as and yet feels less erratic than Thurisaz. Ansuz has helped me unlock my car door several times when I've left the keys inside. I even opened a door with a key that did not match the lock. This was done while speaking the Rune, creating a vibration through speech that helped unleash its power. The term most frequently associated with this type of work is galdr.

> **Galdr** is vocalizing the Runes. You do not have to be a trained singer to do this. I often see it as a place between speaking and singing.

Ansuz is also considered the Rune of Odinn, especially if using the Elder Futhark only. When pulled, it can often signify that Odinn has a hand in the situation or that the querent is Odinn's person. I have also had Gar represent Odinn's influence, but it has a heavier weight to it and very much signifies something that is not only influenced by Odinn but marked by Him in some way.

If calling on the ancestors involved a telephone number, Ansuz would be part of it. On a grand scale, we live in a closed system: the Earth. Because this is the case, the air, although recycled through plants and changed over time, is the same as our ancestors breathed. Our exhalations add to the energy and power of the existing air that our ancestors have added to generation after generation. It is a powerful connector to our ancestors.

In today's hectic world, it is so vital for us to be aware of our energetic hygiene. In many cultures, there is a ceremonial cleansing. In my tradition, we call this recaning. Ansuz can be a great Rune to galdr when cleansing oneself, others, or our homes and physical spaces. If you are so inclined, it can be used in combination with Kenaz (fire), Laguz (water), and Jera (earth) for cleansings using the elements.

> **Recaning** is the cleansing ourselves of the energetic dirt or emotions that can impede our connection to ourselves, others, and the otherworlds.

Another aspect of Ansuz refers to messages. In this instance, it can indicate that a message is trying to be delivered. It tells us to pay attention to the next Rune pulled because it will be the message. Remember, communication in our time can be through email, text, or physical letters delivered to our mailboxes. Traditionally, messages were delivered verbally, by breath. This is not always applicable today, so keep an open mind regarding how the message may be provided.

Hagalaz

Themes & Stories: Hail, Ancestors, Indirect Path, Shit Happens
Deity: Hela

Weather
Forecast
calls for
Rain
Sun
Hail

Always
Looking for the
Next
Storm

Are you
Prepared
Sometimes
Shit Happens
&
you Step in it
not because
you deserved it
Just because

Are You
Choosing to
Stick
Your Tongue
to the
Flag Pole
during a
Lightning Storm

All Hail Hail! Bad joke? It is necessary to have a sense of humor when dealing with some of the more common concepts and ideas of Hagalaz. I have encountered a wide range of meanings over the years.

One of the ideas I often see when Hagalaz shows up is the challenge of the, "Why me?" mentality. It is healthy, I believe, to be reminded that sometimes shit happens. It can be a challenging idea to accept. Accepting this idea means we must accept that bad things can happen to good people. Even more challenging to get is that bad things don't always happen to bad people. Just because someone was a dick doesn't mean they will be dicked right back ... that came out wrong, but you know what I mean.

When we encounter rough waters, we often look for a reason. That is helpful, yes. It is also beneficial to be told, "Don't bother looking." This can keep us from wasting our time looking for a reason. That is a fantastic gift, I believe.

Hagalaz can help signify the need to connect with one's ancestors who may have passed through the gates of Helheim. Not everyone ends up there, but it is like an international airport with flights departing daily for destinations afar. I often will engage the assistance of Hagalaz when asking Hela for time with folks who may be in Her care.

> **Helheim** is the realm of Hel/Hela. It is the Underworld, the place where most of the dead reside.

Hagalaz is one of the Runes that represents the subconscious and what we modernly refer to as "shadow work." Hagalaz can be a deep dive Rune. One journey offered by Hagalaz is that of a long and isolated road through fog and silence. This journey leads into the depths of our Wyrd and can bring to our awareness the very nature of nature. This glimpse into the natural and honest way of things can be frightening, for it shows us that our illusion does not produce life.

> **Shadow Work** should only be undertaken by enlisting the services of a licensed mental health professional. You'll need the support!

Another small but impactful message delivered by Hagalaz is that we are taking the long way. And it is because of our choices, not because someone is making us. Hagalaz, as the Stormbringer, can be cleansing but will send down giant hailstones to beat you into being "clean." This is a rare aspect to surface.

I live on the eastern side of a wide valley with a large lake to the north. Most often, we can see storms coming in from the northwest. I am lucky to see far into the distance, one way of foretelling the future ... okay, the weather for the afternoon. Most of us have experienced everything from hot sunny days to blizzards so cold and dense that seeing your hand in front of your face is impossible.

When we encounter the worst storms, we remember the details and the events leading up to them, like the green hue of the clouds before tornadoes. We learn to prepare for such storms. If we become overly concerned with the next storm, we can become fixated on looking to the horizon, waiting for that storm.

Continuing with this thread, "waiting for the other shoe to drop" is a modern term that shows up frequently when I'm working with folks who have had some serious shit happen in their lives. It is hard to be happy and enjoy the sunshine when one is looking for a storm. The extreme of this occurs when one cloud appears, and that one cloud starts a storm of emotions that lead to the belief that the storm is coming. Simply stated, we do not focus on the present happiness. We focus on the inevitable despair. When this is present, Hagalaz can remind us that while storms are helpful, they also pass. Enjoy the sunny day!

Teiwaz

Themes & Stories: Truth, Justice, Discipline, Honor, Courage, Warrior
Deity: Tyr

Storms of Voices
Puppets
Made Of Socks
Magnets
Pulling
at
You
at the
Needle
of
Your Compass

Show Me The Way
MY
Way
through
the
yanking
pushing
thrashing
of
Others
with
Courage & Honor

Imagine a compass. See the needle pointing North. Feel the surety of that. Now imagine several magnets being placed near the compass. Do you know what happens? The needle gets pulled in a different direction than North. This scenario is one of the ways I see Teiwaz showing up for folks and myself in my experiences.

I am easily excitable! Yes, that way too, but that's not what I'm talking about here. I have a problem saying the word "No." In the past, I believed this was because I didn't want to disappoint anyone. As I grew older and hopefully wiser, the reason for saying no became different. I'm totally screwed if I'm speaking to someone passionate and charismatic about a project or an idea they want me to participate in. Their excitement gets me excited, and before I know it, I've committed to the project. I haven't even checked to see if I have availability on my calendar.

When a dear friend and intuitive tarot reader, Andy, pointed this out to me, he gave me some great advice. Wait to say yes. I can be excited at that moment and never, ever say yes. Walk away and let the excitement settle down. Check my calendar and commitments to see if it is possible. Wait a few days. I can say yes if I am still excited and able after a few days. If I am not, then no harm, no foul.

This would not be such a big deal today to some people. Some might think making and then breaking promises is not a problem. Promises between people would not be taken so lightly if keeping them meant life or death. Looking at the Rune Mannaz, we see that the Runes provide wisdom on building community through relationships and boundaries, which is an essential part of life. When working in a community, if one is constantly breaking their commitments, they would not be seen as reliable and, therefore, would not be supported by the community. They become a strain on the community, not a strength.

There are two concepts in my tradition and worldview that speak to this importance, maegen, and hamingja. Maegen is the ability to make and keep your word. As you can guess, not making and breaking the promise keeps the maegen intact, which is ideal. Hamingja is the power, sometimes referred to as luck, that one gains from the value given to one by the community.

This power is like a bank account. If you want to purchase an item, you can use the money in the account. If the account is empty, then you can not make the purchase. And no, the concept of credit doesn't apply here. When you want to make something happen, this power helps make it happen. Again, you can see how this could be negatively impacted.

Returning to the compass idea, walking away allows us to remove the magnets. It provides for time to recenter and return to our own North. This happens way more than one would think, and the wisdom of Teiwaz helps to point out when someone has lost their North. This happens in relationships and friendships and in the workplace.

I direct folks to centering, grounding, and shielding basics during sessions. These aren't just fluffy New Age terms meant to get us to contemplate breathing. These are good techniques to be able to connect with oneself. This is a place of alignment from which we can begin to be pulled in a direction that can lead us to more fulfillment and peace.

Teiwaz is connected to Tyr, one of the Gods of War, more connected to the ideas of Justice and Truth. He is a warrior who acts from a place of honor and justice, not rage and anger. If we can align our compass with our own truth, as mentioned in the compass idea, we will have begun to develop our own identity as an individual. With Teiwaz and Tyr present in this process, we can see how discipline, courage, perseverance, self-reliance, and mental clarity can emerge. This feels like a military training situation to me, guided by honor.

In terms of war, I have also experienced Teiwaz asking, "If you are the only one left standing on the battlefield, have you truly won the war?"

Eihwaz

Themes & Stories: Balance of Life & Death, Defense, Yew Tree

Yew

As Below
So Above
but
what about the
Liminal Space
of the
Middle

What happens
When
Balance Occurs
True Balance

does
A
Liminal
Balance
between
Life & Death
Create
the Space
to Slip
Between
the
Two

Back in my — if you can believe it — corporate ladder-climbing days, I began my process of remembering Eihwaz even though it wasn't until 10 years later that I saw the Rune. The wisdom of the Runes surfaces like white caps on ocean waves throughout our lives, reminding us that we know more than we can imagine.

I was a regional manager covering seven states in the midsouth of the United States. I was on my way to becoming the next regional vice president. Those days seem so far removed from me now. We would have weekly conference calls to convey all the necessary information for the week. All my colleagues and I dreaded them. I learned to hate them because of the treatment I received from my boss because I do not identify as a straight cis man. Oh, the youth and virility of my twenties — he hated that and didn't want to hire me but was told he had to because I was the most qualified.

He became famous for giving me a hard time. One day, when asked about a project I was working on, I responded that whatever I had missed had "fallen off my plate." He promptly replied without missing a beat, "You better get a bigger plate." At some point, we all laughed and joked about getting that printed on a shirt.

The point of this story is this, if your plate is full, there is no getting a bigger one. You must remove things from the plate to add more.

Eihwaz shows up this way in readings to point out that the client needs to clear off their plate before taking on new projects. It even shows up in questions about relationships. You can't take a new lover if you still smell like the old one. Yes, Eihwaz is a Rune of the balance of life and death, and can have some brilliant modern applications beyond literal life and death.

There are some great depths to be explored in the aspect of it connecting to the Yew tree. I believe there could be some very ritualistic uses that we can only imagine as those ideas have been lost to the exhales of the last storytellers before the conquerors slit their throats. Sit with Eihwaz and ask to be shown what happened around the trunks of the yew trees.

Eihwaz has traditionally been seen as a Rune of defense. This could connect back to the use of the Yew tree in making bows and staves.

There is something to note in the pictograph's design: The balance between the branches and the roots. You can see this by drawing a horizontal line and splitting it into equal parts. This idea coincides with the importance placed upon the roots of Yggdrasil in the Northern Traditions. The three Wells exist there: the Well of Urd, Hvergelmir, and the Well of Mimir. Much happens in the roots to keep the Tree healthy. How are you caring for your roots? Do you care for your roots?

Othila

Themes & Stories: Ancestral Land, Family, Ancestors Hallowed Ground

Now Hollow

No
Blood
No
Bone
No
Heart
to
Fill the Empty Spaces
Left By
Our
Greed
Our
Take
Take
Take

We Must Return
The
Favor
Give
Your
Body
to
The
Dirt

This Rune has a breadth that can refer to all things ancestral and family-related. I frequently talk about our bodies being made up of genetic programming to manifest our hair color and physical build and the stored wisdom of the experiences of our ancestors. And of the Runes. For this reason, I suggest to my clients and students that they quickly become comfortable with being embodied. This is the best way to access this wisdom.

> **Embodied** is a state of being and an aspect of alignment. Embodied is literally the expression of something in a tangible or visible form. For us to be embodied means that we embrace, accept, honor, celebrate, and know our physical form. The body and its processes and drives can be seen as something to shed, overcome and escape. This is far from the truth. Our bodies are the tool we use to interact and communicate with the seen and unseen worlds.

Othila is an access point to connect with our ancestors. The pictograph can be thought of as a human holding a shield. It can be used to mark and bless your property's boundaries. Othila can help you find your own hearth and home. One Rune combination I created and utilize is called An Orphan No More. It combines two Runes, Othila and Teiwaz. Othila represents having a home and hearth of our own that the ancestors grant. Teiwaz represents truth as well as the compass needle guiding our way.

Othila is a Rune that can be an access point when contacting the dead, especially your ancestors. Othila shows up frequently as an indicator that what the other Runes in the casting/reading are discussing is family related. Othila is also a Rune that can be used for grounding and shielding.

Recently, I conducted a general Rune reading for the community that I posted online. I pulled Othila, Ac, and Algiz. The meaning was impactful. We all need each other. We need our close family groups, regardless of whether they are blood. We need to foster relationships with those people. These groups or communities provide protection and shelter, support, and camaraderie. You can see here how Othila flavors and gives context to the message.

If we look at the sigil for Othila, it can be split into several different Rune combinations. The one I am referencing now is that of Othila, comprising three Kenaz Runes. From my own gnosis, I see this connecting to the three Centers of Knowing (intellect, emotion, and instinct). When the three of these are all accessed and used, we can genuinely unlock and access the wisdom held in our bodies. The wisdom passed down to us from our ancestors.

Isa

Themes & Stories: Ice, Blockage, Preservation & Destruction, Glaciers, Standstill

How does one
Connect
with
Isa
in a
Heat Wave

Stillness
Heavy
Stifling
Breath
Taking

Hmmm
Same as Cold

In stillness
We Experience
Our Fears
Isa
has
No Emotion
&
Fear
is
False Danger

calm
still

I always find it fascinating that the Runes of hail, needfire, and ice are lined up together (Hagalaz, Nauthiz & Isa if you were to look at them in their usual sequence.) My whole life has been an exercise in balancing the raging fire of my needs and desires with not only the depths associated with water but also with the immensity and power of it in ice form.

It goes without saying that most people do not seek out guidance when things in their lives are going well. I have encountered many folks who feel they need help. They feel stagnant. They feel stuck. Sometimes these pauses are required to allow for our development to settle, to take a fucking break. I use the following to help as a guide for folks who are in this place.

Imagine yourself on a glacier. If you don't know what one looks like, quickly find a photo and try to picture yourself there. This glacier takes up an entire valley. It is miles long, wide, and very thick. The only sensation you feel is the cold wind caressing your cheeks. It seems like the whole world is standing still. The truth is that the glacier is moving. It is carving out with immense power and weight the valley below. It sculpts the sides of the valley. Rivers are running through and under in some cases. The ice has trapped remnants of past peoples and animals in its grasp. There is much happening under your feet. You are not at a standstill.

This aspect of Isa is essential because I want everything right now. It has only been within the context of developing my psychic gifts and shamanic practices that I have indeed come to embrace and look forward to the times when I can rest, catch my breath, and allow my body and consciousness to integrate the remembered wisdom stored therein.

Isa can be an incredible Rune to work with when you are anxious or overwhelmed. I will galdr Isa while sitting still to help center myself in these times.

Ice can be like a mirror. The reflective surface can show us the things we have locked away. In some cases, it is not only a reflection but the client frozen in the ice, and the distance from the edge of the ice is relative to how deeply buried the aspect is. I have encountered this with clients who have repressed needs and desires. The image in the reflection represents the aspect of the client. For instance, we may see the part of ourselves that is carefree and fun loving presented wearing shorts and a t-shirt. Staying with this idea, Isa may be able to help us preserve these aspects so that we may engage with them later.

An idea was recently shared with me by Sophia Fate-Changer, another Rune Walker. I'm very excited to see where this takes me. Ice can form bridges during the winter. Over wide rivers. Even between continents. Isa as a bridge builder. This excites me.

Inguz

Themes & Stories: Sacrifice, Sexuality, Fecundity, Initiation
Deity: Freyr, Ingvi Frey

Sacrificial Blood
Never Spilled Carelessly
Always Thoughtfully
Sprayed
from the
Fresh Wounds
Opened
by
Sacred
Blades
to
Ensure
Next
Year's
Mouth Will Be Fed
Bellies Full
Fields Overflowing
with
Golden Wheat

Passage Paid

Let's discuss sacrifice. Inguz holds much wisdom about sacrifice. It is the Rune connected to Freyr or Ingvi Frey. Every year around harvest time, when it's time to prepare the fields for winter, Freyr is sacrificed. His skin is opened, and his blood flows freely and sweetly onto the fields. The dark earth soaks up His life to give life next season. Freyr offers this sacrifice willingly and knowingly. He knows the sacrifice must be provided. He is the one to give it year after year, season after season.

Inguz can be marked on anything that is to be sacrificed or marked as sacred. It is an honorable thing to be sacrificed. It is essential to be aware of what is being sacrificed and its intention. Freyr is sacrificed because life requires a living sacrifice. When asked to offer something as a sacrifice, what would your process of choosing it be?

I've facilitated plenty of rituals and seen many offerings. Over the years, I have seen (and personally offered) store-bought food and other items. I have tried to shift my process and make something for the offering. No matter how little the offering, it means more if made by my hands.

Fortunately for Gerda and Freya, Freyr comes back every year. It does not make it any easier or create less mourning and wailing to know he will be back, though. In fact, mourning and wailing are part of the sacrifice. We have not genuinely sacrificed if the thing we have sacrificed doesn't bring us to tears accompanied by mourning.

Initiation is another aspect of Inguz that I want to discuss. Initiatory rites often require sacrificing one way of being to step into another. This falls within the parameters of sacrifice and often represents that clients are going through some sort of initiation themselves. Most clients need to find out what is causing the resistance to help them let go and move through the opening to the other side.

I experience Inguz as an intensely sexual Rune. It can speak to the fecundity of spring. It is the natural force behind spreading legs and seeds. It is raw. It is unfiltered and explosive. It is the little deaths that have the potential to create life. And if not life, living.

Yr

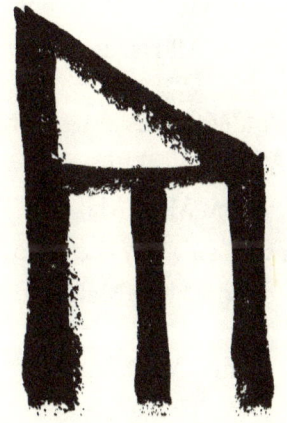

Themes & Stories: Mastery, Focus, Leveling Up, Craftsman, Death to Bring Life
Deity: Skadi

Much Is Required
to Survive
in the
Snowy North
Hunting is Different
Tracking is Different
All Harder

You Must Become More
You Can't Buy the Bow
You Must Make It
You Can't Buy the Arrow
You Must Make It

You Must Know
The Wind
The Bow
The Arrow
Intimately
They Must Be
Part of You

I often compare a soldier to an assassin as my jumping-off point for this Rune. A regular foot soldier has been trained in the basics of combat and has gained enough proficiency to do the job adequately. At the other end of this comparison, the assassin has the same skills as the soldier and many more. The assassin has received additional training and experience in long-distance rifle use, other languages, or martial arts. The focus needed for this is where I begin with Yr.

Yr is connected to the archer, bow, and arrow. And is the archer, the bow, and the arrow. And is the knowledge and skill to make the bow and arrow. And is the knowledge and skill to accurately hit a moving target and kill it with one arrow. Yr is the knowledge and skill to survive in the cold north, where snowfall betrays your position of hiding from your prey and leads a predator straight to you.

In my modern-day readings and associations, Yr suggests that the client needs to attend some continuing education or is currently engaged in it. It frequently conveys that it is time to take charge and master your craft. It is time to focus with dedication to your development and understanding. Sometimes this is a tricky concept for us. I know that with my upbringing in the public school system of the United States, the focus was on making me a well-rounded individual. This translates well into the phrase, "jack of all trades, master of none." This is the opposite of the wisdom Yr holds.

Recently, I became initiated as a winged shaman. It was a beautiful experience and one that encompassed years of hard work. After I returned home from my journey and had specific images tattooed onto my body, I sat with my set of Runes and began divining my next steps. I asked Odinn for his opinion and guidance. The response was Stan and Yr together. "It is time to become the Master." Yr is becoming a master.

Pertho

Themes & Stories: The Mysteries, Risk, Unknown, Gaming

Deity: Nornir (Urd, Verdandi, Skuld,) Mimir

Two
Things

1
Good Times
Build Bridges
Between Us

2
Risk & Movement
Yes
and
Sometimes
We Must Be Still
&
Sit in the Pot
as it
Comes to a Boil

Pertho is the keeper of the mysteries. Or at least the doorway to them. Maybe even the shapeless and limitless container of the idea of mysteries. Was that confusing enough?

Sometimes it is difficult with modern language to explore these concepts that transcend words. When I began facilitating classes about the Runes, I quickly realized that the keystone to accessing their wisdom was our ability to know, rather than receive, confirmation — that what each of us experiences is true for each of us. How is this possible? It reminded me of the early days of my relationship with the Runes.

I began by trying to memorize the names that matched the glyph. Then I would move on to memorizing the keywords or concepts. It was an extremely frustrating thing. I couldn't seem to do this. I am capable of memorization and did quite well in school and business, meaning there were no cognitive challenges impeding my ability to memorize. Then, I realized that I had been trying to access wisdom via my brain power only. Silly Kenn!

We have physical bodies to interact with the physical world and help us translate experiences with the unseen. Some of the most brilliant advice I've ever received was this: If your mind tells you it doesn't understand or can't comprehend what is being presented, trust it. Thank you, Theresa Carmody, Celtic shaman, marriage & family therapist, LMFT.)

As mentioned earlier, we have three Centers of Knowing. Each of these can be experienced as its own Pertho. Also, I see the physical body as Pertho and the wisdom inside held by genetic DNA as the Mysteries.

Sometimes Pertho asks us to go internally and find the answers. We are meant to plumb our own depths for wisdom, endarkenment. I like viewing Pertho through this lens while placing the Rune in the context of the Well that holds all of the threads, the Well of Urd. If we look into this well, we see our reflection. We hold the key. The connection also concerns the Nornir, so I have occasionally experienced Pertho as Their presence or influence in someone's life.

On a far less serious note, Pertho says, "Don't take life too seriously." Take some risks and chances. You cannot always know what the outcome will be. Where's the fun in that?

I have also had it represent the need for my client to make friends and have fun. There is a thread of community that runs through this Rune. It speaks to the bonds created through laughter and play.

Stan

Themes & Stories: Time/Perspective, Foundations, Portals/Gateways

Deity: Ymir

Stone Cold
Hot Stones
Standing Stones
Stone Circles
Stoned
KeyStone
Stone Cold Silent
Moving at a Glacial Pace
or Slower

Indicator
Watcher
Storyteller
If You Are Patient

Stan often presents itself as the indicator that what is happening is central or foundational to the situation in readings. There are more than a few ways to utilize the Runes for divination. If I am pulling one only to answer a question, and it is Stan, I pull another using the philosophy above. Stan is there to tell us to pay good fucking attention to what comes next because it's imperative. It is more than an answer to my question, which may have been presented superficially. To get to the bottom of this, we need to go deeper.

More recently, I have begun to see it concerning people's spiritual development. In this regard, the main message is that there is a need to slow down and listen. The lifespan of a stone is far beyond our ability to comprehend. Because their lives move at a much slower, or what to us seems slower, pace, their communication may be as a super-slow motion sound. Because this is often the case when receiving vocalized communication from stones, we must be able to sit very still and quietly for periods to understand what is being said.

I love the mountains and can be obsessed with searching for stones. I grew up in the Oquirrh Mountains, hiking, hunting, collecting firewood and pine nuts, and exploring them. I grew up with my father and grandfather pointing out each of the mines and telling me stories about them.

I remember hiking one summer day near what was once a busy mining town, Jacob City. I was looking for downed aspen trees. I was high in altitude, and aspen groves, pine trees, and some thick scrub oak surrounded the path. I came around a slight bend on the hillside path, and rising up between the trees was a rock outcropping.

Some places have a special "density" that is different from what we would consider normal spaces. This place was one of those places. Here, I felt that density and a deep sense of reverence. I've also experienced this feeling in Ireland at giant rock cairns and megalithic monuments.

In my explorations with Stan, I've been shown that it is also a way or path. I could use the word portal here as a better descriptor, but it feels too fluffy and doesn't command the respect needed for the path walking it may provide. Much the same way I experienced those stones to be different from mundane space, I've felt Stan the same. This is as a path walking marker or entrance. Stan is a way to the ways.

Nauthiz

Themes & Stories: Needfire, Friction, Focus, Sexual Lust, No

Need Fire
Lust Fire
Friction Fire

Must Start
the Fire

Why can we
Not
put down
the Sticks
After
the Fire
Sparked
Started
Must
We Burn Ourselves
in the
Flames

Know When

Enjoy the Warmth
of
Your
Work
Your
Friction
Your
Desire

Have you ever been taken to the edge of desperation? Have you ever been so fucking horny that you could not think straight? Have you ever been so hungry that you are beyond hungry — you're ravenous?

Think about these questions again after removing your idea of want and desire. This is far deeper than that. It's not about being horny. It's not about the physical pain of having "blue balls." It is the pain from a stomach empty for weeks — so empty that you begin to eat your fingertips. Fortunately for you, if you can access this book and are reading it, your Nauthiz need probably does not manifest in that way. It is for some around the world, though.

Nauthiz is a fire Rune. It represents aspects of fire and how we interact with it. I have encountered Nauthiz, as many other writers of these words have before. One of my favorites is when Ingrid Kincaid speaks about the need for friction. You can't oil the sticks before rubbing them together. This will not create the friction necessary to start fires. Brilliant!

Many years ago, I attended a gathering/celebration of sexual freedom. This weekend's event was filled with folks from all over the United States and maybe some international folks. What I loved about this event was that it accepted and embraced the idea that sex is an essential part of life. It wasn't a giant orgy, although that would have been fun. The hotel was very cool, and the room doors were painted with chalkboard paint so we could write on them. I rolled up to the door of my room with my suitcase. I opened the door, and without delay, I grabbed the red piece of chalk and marked Nauthiz on my door. I wanted to experience that lusty, consuming passion that fire and Nauthiz can share. It was an excellent weekend! And the hotel did not burn down.

I also want to share with you one of my embodied moments with Nauthiz that manifested in a different way. It is not sexual in nature … although I have had many in addition to that weekend, I spoke about above.

Since I became my own boss more than a decade ago in this world of careers and work, I have tried to pay only cash and not work with the credit system. This means that until recently, I have been attempting to pay cash to not incur high-interest rates by borrowing money as I write my paycheck. It is much harder to get loans when you work for yourself in a small business. I'm sure there is a better way, and I'm also sure that finance is not my gift.

In the Spring of 2022, I felt I would need to make some extra cash or at least get a "normal" job to show income because my car was starting to break down. I also wanted a few things paid off more quickly, so I got a job working overnights.

I can't make this next part up. My car broke down. My motorcycle broke down. My father's truck that I borrowed broke down. I was completely at a loss. Some of this involved my preparations for oathing to the Gods and becoming a shaman of the Northern Traditions. That is a whole separate story, though.

I will fast-forward the story three months to my moment of illumination. I had my new-to-me car. I had the things paid off I wanted to pay off. I decided to keep this job for my income, for now. During these months, I worked 40+ hours overnights, worked with my clients, prepared for my initiation, and volunteered for a local non-profit. I was wiped out most of the time.

One night around 9 p.m., just before we went on break, I was folding a cardboard box, readying it to ship an order, when I saw it. In my mind, I saw the story I've told clients many times when Nauthiz has shown up in their readings. I saw my hands holding two wooden sticks and rubbing them together to start a fire. And the fire was already going. I was rubbing sticks in the middle of the fire burning myself. I shook my head in complete disbelief that I had missed this. I felt a release of all the stress I had been holding and was light as a feather. I promptly offered my resignation and went home to nurse my burns and sleep.

Nauthiz sometimes signals that we are still rubbing the sticks together even after the fire is burning. I have experienced this in other situations with clients as well. Once, it represented fulfilling goals that were not what the client desired. In this case, the client continued to work, thinking they may feel fulfillment someday. The goals they worked toward were what I call The White Picket Fence. The American Dream. The things we are told to want because they will make us happy. There is no one solution or way to happiness.

Gebo

Themes & Stories: Gift, Exchange, Crossroads, Balance

It is a
Gift
to
Cherish
that we have
Folks
Around
Us
to Share in
Good times
Bad times
Bountiful and Lean times
to keep them
We
Must
Honor
True Balance
of
Exchange
True Imbalance
of
Exchange

Did you ever go to the circus as a kid? Do you remember the tightrope walkers? Imagine the tightrope walkers 40 feet above you, the crowd watching in awe. Their mouths open, and their muscles tense as the tightrope walker places one foot onto the small, taut cable. Everyone holds their collective breath. The walker carefully sets their other foot from the solid surface onto the rope, then turns around and grabs the white pole firmly with both hands. If we look closely, we can see the various muscles of the leg contract and release. The abdominal muscles tighten, and the spine lengthens. Every muscle participates in a dance. A dance to keep this daring highwire artist on that tiny cable. This reminds me of one of the ways I experience Gebo.

In modern times we hear about finding or obtaining balance. This often applies to the concept of work and home life. I believe Gebo to be a different, or maybe more profound, balance than is often cited as Gebo's meaning. Yes, it can just mean "Gift," and it can mean so much more. In my workings with clients, as I have read and interpreted their Rune castings, Gebo often symbolizes the imbalance they are experiencing due to not giving enough or giving too much.

For example, I live on my family land, which has been in the family for four generations. We have difficulty growing things here because the climate and soil are challenging. The topsoil was brought in after a toxic cleanup of lead-filled soil was removed. The town was built on mine tailings. The new topsoil has dried up and blown away, leaving us dust, pebbles, and plants that most people may find irritating and unwanted.

Three badgers were killed on the highway near my home a few years ago. I had only seen one badger growing up, far from civilization. These creatures were being forced from their habitat by the emergence of gravel pits. I picked up their bodies and buried them in my backfield to honor them. After a few years, I dug up one of them to see how the decomposition was progressing. As I dug down, the soil was rich and dark. There were a few bones and fur but primarily rich, dark soil.

The soil had been depleted, and nothing had been put back. Yes, we could have applied chicken and horse manure, which we have in the past. What struck me was that our bodies are pumped full of chemicals and put in asbestos boxes when we die. We do not actually return to the soil to be broken down and used to feed the organisms that create the rich soil for the plants to grow. These plants feed us and the animals we eat. There is a cycle here, and we are dangerously out of balance.

I see this imbalance in communities, as well. It can be challenging for folks to find a community they feel comfortable in and want to join. This ties into one's maegen and hamingja. Maegen is the ability to make and keep your word. Hamingja is the power, sometimes referred to as luck, that one gains from the value given to one by the community. Having a community of folks who depend on each other is good. One day we may help someone with their projects, and on another day, they will repay us by helping us. This dance of give and take binds communities together through honored obligation and respect.

The balance sought by the tightrope walker and the communities I just mentioned is not a static place or end goal. This balance is ever-changing and flowing. Once the tightrope walker achieves balance, something else shifts, and their muscles repeatedly continue the dance of finding balance. The same is true for communities. Honorable obligation and debt are part of the beauty of Gebo. The phrase "nothing comes free" is accurate, and Gebo can help us more fully appreciate and understand the nature of our relationships with everything around us.

This may be an excellent time to think of Fehu and your relationship with your things. Do you use everything you have? Do you have clothes in the closet with the tags still on them? Do you have multiples of an item? Do you recycle things or just toss them aside? Just some questions to ponder. If Fehu and Gebo come up in a reading together, depending on the context given by the question, they can signify hoarding or not caring for oneself properly.

Fehu

Themes & Stories: Value, Wealth, Management of Resources, Money, Self-Worth
Deity: Freya

beginnings & sparks
tails & trails
value & worth
healthy herds
hoards
if I have no worth
then I am not worthy
I must value myself
my spark
my list
drive
passion
penis
genetic material
ability
inability
If I am worth nothing to myself
I am worth nothing to Them

Fehu is the first Rune in the Elder Futhark and Angle Saxon Futhorc. Fehu is the beginning. It is the first spark. In these realms, and depending on other Runes near it in the reading, it can mean a new relationship or new business, or legal ventures. The Runes are interconnected and form more complex ideas when they pair together. Fehu can represent abundance and inspiration.

Fehu is concerned with wealth and value. In some ways, Fehu ties back to the proper management and value of a herd of animals. In today's world, this can be stocks, land, or a simple business-promoting post on social media. The idea is that we must be in a balanced relationship with our possessions. We cannot put a new lamb and its mother out to summer pasture without protecting them and ensuring they are cared for. Similarly, we must tend to social media posts that aim to gain clients and/or income.

Another aspect is that of the modern storage unit. We become possessed by our possessions. We pay every month to store items that we rarely interact with. Our garage is full of boxes moving around the space because no one can get rid of them. The objects represent people, places, and experiences we wish to remember. Maybe in some way, this leads to the question, "What value do you place on the past over the present?"

To continue the ideas of worth and value, Fehu can help with one's self-worth. I believe this is also where Fehu and Freya can partner quite well when it comes to finding one's own value as a sexual being, as a being with passion and value. Most of us do not value ourselves as sexual entities. We only value ourselves based on being desired by others.

This Rune can be one to partner with when searching for your talents and gifts. Fehu can help us use them in ways that allow them to be fully expressed. Fehu can also be present in money matters such as constructing a new income plan.

Berkana

Themes & Stories: Growth, Nurturing, Discernment, Mother
Deity: Frigga, Jord

We Can Not Fathom
The Title
Mother
Without
Love
Woven
Into It

Yet Without It
It
Must
Be

Culling
&
Nurturing
These
Are Not Love

They Are Nature

They Are Survival
Our
Survival
Your
Survival
My
Survival

It took me a decade to realize that one of the greatest gifts of Berkana is the ability to remove emotion from the decision-making process. While it is the Rune of the Mother regarding growth and nurturing, it is also about discernment without emotion.

Berkana often appears and asks my clients to determine what to take and what to get rid of in their lives. In this aspect, it works well with Eihwaz when one is trying to figure out what is outdated and needs to be shed. Berkana reminds us that the goal is life and survival of ourselves, our family, and the community. We sometimes have it a little too easy. We do not think about the cost of sustaining something. If we want it, we get it. We need to think about the long-term strain it may place on our resources or community.

On a more individual level, when this Rune shows up in readings, it can let me know that the client is making decisions based on their emotions, and that needs to change. It indeed was an eye-opener for me. Remove the feeling and allow the facts to make the decision. It may be a hard but necessary shift in awareness for us to create. Emotions are not bad. Sometimes, they should not be part of the decision-making process.

Along this same path, I think Berkana warns us to "Manifest responsibly!" If you are the mother of an idea, project, or similar, you must either care for or cull it. This is excellent advice when planning and forming stages of anything new. Berkana asks if we have the time and resources to see this through until it can stand independently. Berkana asks if we really want to commit to our creations. Berkana invites us to consciously participate in the reality of a situation, not just the dream.

Os

Themes & Stories: Breath, Relationship with Breath, Manifesting, Storytelling, Estuary

Breath
First Breath
Last Breath
Deep Breath

Creation
Destruction
Laughter
Wailing
Seduction
Comfort

Each Breath
A Weapon of Mass Destruction
or
A Weapon of Mass Creation

The Power of A God
Held in Each
Exhale

Os is the Rune of the Storyteller and the relationship with the breath that creates and weaves the stories.

Growing up, we would joke about the need to wear hip-waders or bring a shovel to family gatherings. If you are unfamiliar with those terms, let me put it bluntly. My family can weave some wicked bullshit stories if gone unchecked. Sometimes, the depth of the bullshit can get deep enough to need hip-waders to walk around or a shovel to dig yourself out. That is just one aspect of this thread of Os.

In one of its aspects, Os represents the relationship and responsibility we have with our words. To understand the power of Os is to be responsible for not only the creation but also the destruction caused by the vibration of one's vocal cords. I may have thought that saying affirmations to myself in the mirror every morning was silly, but it has power. What you choose to say and how you say it is of utmost importance. This can affect your maegen and hamingja dramatically. Remember, maegen is the ability to make and keep your word and hamingja is the power, sometimes referred to as luck, that one gains from the value given to one by the community.

When I think of Os, I usually picture giving speeches or telling stories around a campfire. I eat this Rune before I give presentations or teach classes. I have even carved it into a ring I wear during readings, classes, or other situations when I need control and power in my voice. Os is a good Rune to galdr as a warm-up for your voice before the above activities.

Occasionally, I will be shown another reference for Os. The image is of an estuary. I do not live near the ocean or water where I can experience high and low tides. I have witnessed it in my journeys, though. One image I understand without explanation is that of a human trying to launch a boat. While in Ireland, I noticed that the high and low tide times are routinely a part of the local information. Sometimes we get stuck in the mud trying to launch our boats (ideas and plans) because the tide is out. Paying attention to timing is crucial. When the tide is high, moving the heavy boat out is much easier because the water does the work. This aspect of Os is a little lesser known but has been very appropriate in guiding me to the correct interpretation for clients.

Wunjo

Themes & Stories: Joy, Light, "Higher Self"
Deity: Frigg

Reach
Down
to go
Higher
You are
Deity
connected
joy
madness
Ecstasy
Life
able to
Receive
Where is
Your
Antenna

"Higher self" is an interesting term we've adopted today. I'm not in love with it. In fact, I think it can be detrimental to us. Words are potent spells, often carelessly cast in every direction. The term most likely does not mean to separate us from our bodies. Still, after owning a metaphysical/spiritual retail store, I can safely say that some people genuinely see that "higher self" as existing outside themselves.

My upbringing in Mormonism conditioned me to believe that the guiding voice in me was delivered by the grace of that god when I became a church member. This is just simply not true. No wonder I had a lot of deprogramming to do to liberate myself from that mindset. I still have a long way to go.

Wunjo is a Rune signifying joy and, on the other end of the spectrum, madness. It is a state of being. A vibration that can cause either sensation — and both, for if you're mad/crazy, you can still feel joy. That's quite the thought, isn't it?

I conducted a Soul Map reading for a client the same day I wrote this. This deep reading left the client feeling drained. A primary focus of the reading was the lack of equal reciprocity, and after years of this pattern, they developed a bitter attitude toward others. As you have clearly experienced, I do not always present the Runes in the order they appear in the futhark/futhorc. However, looking at the Runes Gebo, and Wunjo in their usual futhark/futhorc order reminds us that through relationships of equality, we can gain joy.

Wunjo can be a good focus if one is trying to open their connection to commune with the divine. It occurs when we find that part of ourselves that is divine. I see it as a key — not a key to a door leading somewhere else, but a key that finds the sacred that exists in each of us. We can connect to the greater divine by finding that divine part.

So many of us today are engaged in what is commonly referred to as "shadow work." Wunjo can be asked to partner in this process to give a little light and joy to someone who may be heavy with grief, sadness, or some similarly emotionally difficult situation.

Calc

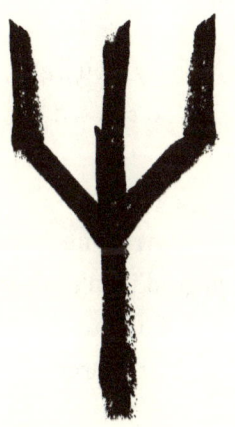

Themes & Stories: Sacred Quest, Fulfillment, Honoring
Deity: Nornir

2022

Deeper Than Your
Greatest Desire
It is
Your Greatest Fulfillment

May You Be
So Blessed
that
The Two
Are One
Oh And Don't Forget
To Pour a
Little Dram
in
Gratitude
to the Roots & Norns
to the Ancestors & Others

2019

The Norns
They stirred me
They steered me
They help me find
They help me discover
my golden ticket
my orgasm
my climax
my wholeness
to honor my ancestors
to honor my progeny
my gods
to share the weight of life
of living life
of eating
working
drinking
playing
fucking
drinking more
loving harder

share the wealth
share the hearth
share the fire
drink from the wells in the roots
in your roots drink
drink from the same wells
they came from
they drank from
they returned to
in death
cheers
drink up and don't forget
pour some out in gratitude
in thanks
in honor

A storm was rolling in as I began laying out my thoughts. The wind blew fresh cool air through my windows, and I felt the tiniest raindrops on my skin. I thought of the shape of the Rune, its signature. I generally experience it with the three prongs pointed up, but the image that rolled through my head was one of lightning.

Two funny things: 1) The first time I encountered Calc, it was with the three prongs pointed down and felt very much like two legs and a cock, and 2) last Saturday morning, I asked Thor and his mother, Jord to ease up on his stormy advances, so that our Saturday market would be dry (and, thankfully, it was).

Calc has, of course, many facets like a well-cut diamond or intricately woven tapestry. My first profound experience with Calc was in Ireland. We were staying at a house on a hill overlooking Rathmullen, a small town in the north, and Lough Swilly, which led to the open sea. I pulled Calc from my Rune bag and knew immediately that I was to go out back and fashion an altar to the Nornir. Yes, I know. I just said I experienced it as a male with two legs and a cock.

This is the beauty of the Runes and fostering relationships with these beings. That time I experienced prongs pointing down. In Ireland, the prongs were up this time, and there was no mistaking that the Nornir — Urd, Verdandi, and Skuld — had somehow been part of this Rune pulling. This encounter has led to many interactions with the Nornir over the past years. I have learned different lessons every time. So, I now have that connection to Calc and that reference to draw from.

The Nornir seem to be aloof. That may be the word. They are in charge of weaving the great tapestry of life, so they're busy. They have doled out information to me, and I'm grateful because it always seems to have been at a time when I needed a breakthrough, something that really shifted my life. Along those lines, I have had Calc appear in readings to show that a god has marked the client.

The few times this happened, the client confirmed this was true. The connection between a god and the client was one that, in each situation, was consensual.

Let's shift gears and look at another thread in this rich weave. Calc can signify someone's "holy grail," so to speak. I'm using words I don't love but convey the appropriate message. A "holy grail" is someone's greatest desire and fulfillment. In readings, there is usually a Rune that falls near Calc that helps clarify their desires, which is helpful.

I recently had a combination of Runes that told the story of a person who needed to find what that fulfillment was for them. I love this because it gets to the heart of my goal: Sovereignty for all! Self-government, self-containment.

I went through a period of deconstruction when I had to embody the idea that life is what I make of it, my choice. It's not in the hands of someone else or some deity (for most of us). That was a fucking rough period because, in the beginning, all I could grasp was the gravity of the phrase, "Besides propagating the species, life has no meaning except that which I give it."

That's heavy. That can cause feelings of being lost. What you have to do then is take yourself by the balls or cunt whatever you have and make the life you want. Try new things. Figure out what you like and don't like. Figure out what you want! You are responsible for your own fulfillment.

I have had Calc show me that the client's cup is half full, full, or empty. This means exactly what it says. For example, one of my clients gave too much and never took the time to fill her cup back up. Simple concept, but one that most of us struggle with.

Let's finish by chatting about the balance of sacrificing, honoring, and respecting. It probably needs more than one word to describe it. Calc asks us to look at how we honor those we are in a relationship with, specifically regarding our survival and existence. Do you take a drink from the cup of mead and pass it to the next person without forgetting to pour some out to honor your ancestors and Gods? Or do you drink the whole thing and pass an empty cup on? What are your feelings about gratitude? Are you grateful? Should you be grateful? What should you be thankful for? These questions are so essential for us to answer. Calc is a beautiful Rune.

Kenaz

Themes & Stories: Inner Fire, Inner Knowing, Yes, Truth

The Light
The Hearthfire
The Torch
The Illumination
The Magnetic Pull
What's in front of me
To the sides
To the rear
Above & Below
Help me
Be
See
Feel
That
I
May
Know

Kenaz is the inner fire, the inner knowing that comes from your core being. Fire isn't always the best word to describe this concept. It goes deeper. It can be a magnetic pull toward people, places, or things that align or resonate with your core being. It can be a resounding "Yes!" affirmation.

A fundamental way to look at Kenaz is as a torch to see in the dark. Using that description, I feel trapped in the binary of light and dark — the binary of good and bad. Outside of that statement, Kenaz is the sense that allows us to navigate without always relying on our other more tangible and physical senses.

In my podcast, Rune Walking in Modern Times, I begin some episodes with the phrase, "Welcome to My Hearth, My Fire." This inner fire is the fire I'm talking about. This fire is unique to each of us and is fed differently by each of us. It is a sacred fire that you must tend to. This fire of yours is a fire that keeps you warm, feeds you, and provides illumination.

As a boy scout, we would put many different things on the fire to see what would happen. We peed on it. That smell is unpleasant. We burned shredded pieces of rubber tires. That produced a lot of black smoke. Vegetation that was too green didn't burn well and created a lot of smoke. Use discretion when deciding what you will use to fuel your fire.

As I spoke about in the Uruz chapter, the concept of endarkenment applies here. This "knowing" that Kenaz represents is an embodied experience, and Kenaz is also the wisdom gained once our bodies process the knowledge. In many New Age circles, we are presented with the idea that genuinely spiritual experiences are outside our bodies. I believe that is just not true. Only when we are aligned and embodied can we experience life more fully.

This is the perfect place to speak about UPG, unverified personal gnosis. We must begin to listen to the Gods again and work with them. Their guidance and wisdom have been delivered to us for millennia via those with the gifts and abilities to cross over into the otherworlds, those who can directly commune with the Gods and other beings or spirits. This hasn't changed. Our interactions with this process have changed. Kenaz can help us distinguish between thoughts in our heads and genuine communication from the Gods, ancestors, and other beings.

We receive Their stories, guidance, and wills in this modern renewal of our relationships with the Gods, spirits, and ancestors. This information is only sometimes found or verifiable in surviving texts from ancient times. We must remember that our traditions were oral. Those oral traditions and stories put to scant surviving texts were written observations of the customs lacking in the contextual information necessary for understanding. The past should inform our worldviews. As I have mentioned, the past is only one voice in the conversation. If we allow for this to be the only voice, we risk repeating the cycle exemplified by the spread of any "One True" religious practice. Writings can be altered to fit the vanities of the controlling group of people.

One fantastic thing about living in the modern era is that more and more folks are having similar experiences with the Gods, and we can connect remotely. Individually, we have experiences that ancient texts cannot verify. But! With increasing frequency, we can ascertain them because others have similar experiences. One caveat here: I don't believe we need to have all communications verified by others. The ancient seers, healers, and shaman folk did not have this. We must be able to access our own Kenaz to know what is right for us.

Know Your Path is a phrase I use. It has nothing to do with a road. This phrase is about knowing how you will move through life. Know your ethics. Know your values. Allow them to change over time and evolve as you grow and evolve. Know what your alignment feels like. Stay in that alignment. From here, your inner knowing is easy to access, listen to, and feel.

Laguz

Themes & Stories: Flow, Water, Energy Work

Body
Flow
Container
Contained
Shifting through the
Cracks
Crevices
Valleys
of
Bodies
Celestial
Terrestrial
Movement
Constant
Dammed
Not
Forever

I Step into
The
Stream
to Catch
a Thread
Never
The
Same
Moment
Twice

The Rune of water teaches us about flow. For so many years, my life was planned right down to the minute. And if there wasn't a plan, I threw one together and kept busy, kept moving. There can be a flow in that, for sure. It was just not a sustainable one after so many years.

One of the vivid impressions I received of Laguz during a meditation long ago was that of grounding into water. I was shown the image of a house built on firm ground. The following image was of a house floating on water. A giant wave came, and the house flexed with the rise and fall of the wave. It wasn't consumed or destroyed.

I didn't get it at first. It took me a minute to discern the point: We can learn to ground into the ebb and flow of water just as we ground into the firm earth. My mind was blown, and I broke through a doorway that led to breakthroughs in what I thought possible.

More recently, during a reading, I experienced the image of my client digging a trench from their home high in the mountains to her family's home on the coast. This was all to send a message to them. The funny thing was that a river already existed that flowed past her home and ended up at her family's home on the coast. Often we try to force the flow of things into our impatient timelines and shortsighted plans. There is much energy around us, from the moon's influence on our powers of creation to the seasonal wisdom held in the growth cycle of plants.

I will also experience Laguz as a representation of energy work such as reiki or shamanic energy healing practices. Laguz is a Rune I galdr when I encounter blockages that need to be broken through or get the current flowing better when it is sluggish. Ansuz can be added to this for more strength.

Laguz also signifies a connection to the moon and its cycles. This has been presented in readings to indicate the need for the client to keep track of their emotions, energy levels, etc., for a complete lunar calendar. This tracking helps them to understand their own cycles. I'm not talking about menstrual cycles, per se. This is about knowing our patterns to schedule things appropriately and encounter less resistance. For example, I cannot plan many things for the month leading up to my birthday. My energy levels are lower during this time, and I will only become more frustrated and tired. Knowing this helps me plan accordingly.

Skills

"This shit isn't Norse!" This is what some of you may be thinking. "Grounding. Centering. Shielding. That's for those fluffy folks!" Although it may be true that these are not implicitly related to the Northern Traditions texts, they are skills that anyone can utilize to help with self-mastery and interpersonal skills.

It would also be irresponsible of me to exclude some safety training when I have clearly written from a point of view that includes experiences as a psychic and shaman crossing over to and working with beings from other worlds. Will everyone who reads this book try to contact the Runes, gods, or ancestors? No. Will everyone who tries be able to? No. For those who do try, do not attempt without first mastering the following concepts or similar.

Allow me to refresh your memory from a section of the book called Predator and Prey...

"Let me get straight to the point. Humans are not at the top of the food chain. We can get fucked up by things in this physical world and the unseen otherworlds that are bigger and stronger. "

Let us not become a cautionary tale. Please, do not "fuck around and find out!"

Centering

One of the keys to successful development, spiritual or otherwise, is the ability to center oneself. Centering is the act of achieving a state of alignment. Centering creates a calm attitude, body, and emotional state.

Centering results in the ability to distinguish your own life force and energy from that of others. This energy of others can be productive or not. No matter what the impact, our goal is to hear our own voices and desires, unaffected by the will of others.

Imagine a hectic day. The list of tasks and appointments is longer than the day itself. You are going a hundred miles per hour, and the whirlwind of to-do items surrounding you is even faster. That's a lot to balance, and your energy is spinning around you. During times like this, you may need to pause and regroup, gather your thoughts and ideas, and breathe. That is centering.

The idea is to bring all those things spinning around you either back into you, if they are yours, or send them back to where they came from. Bringing everything to a standstill will help you to focus on the present task and not be distracted. This aids our ability to be present in each moment, interaction, and decision.

During centering practice, you may find that you have an excess of or require more energy. This is where grounding comes in, which is why it is the next section. Let's look at one way to center yourself.

Find a calm place with silence, or use headphones to remove distracting sounds. This will become irrelevant as you grow more capable of eliminating sounds from your awareness. If you're at work, this may be a janitorial closet. If at home with a house full of rambunctious kids and spouses, this may be the laundry room — no one wants to help with that chore.

Find a comfortable seated position (lying down works well, but you may take a nap instead).

If you feel comfortable close your eyes and place your hand on your lower abdomen. Pick a point on the wall to focus your attention if you feel uncomfortable closing your eyes. As you inhale, push your hand outward by expanding the lower abdomen. The goal is to breathe deeply and relax the shoulders and neck, which tend to be tense as we raise and lower our shoulders in rushed breathing.

Try the four-fold breath pattern. Some practitioners find it easy to envision drawing a box during this. Everything will be done by counting to four. Begin by inhaling for four counts. Hold that breath for four counts. Exhale for four counts. Hold that for four counts. Repeat.

This practice does not have a specific time allotment. I have experienced it for as little as one minute with success. If your mind wanders away and begins thinking about your to-do list, gently guide yourself back to focusing on your breath. It can help to make your to-do list before you sit down to center yourself. This gives you confidence that nothing will be forgotten.

One of the Runes that I love for centering is Isa, the Rune of Ice. I begin with the breathing technique listed above. As my breathing settles in, I softly galdr the word Isa. I visualize a needle-thin icicle entering the top of my head. It slowly moves down the center of my body until it exits my perineum. The icicle continues to lower between my legs to the floor; my vision is of me standing, even if I'm sitting.

Once the icicle has gone through the center, I imagine it expanding and growing thicker as I inhale and exhale. I continue this until the icicle encompasses my body. As it expands, I see it freezing in place, the things whirling around me. This stops their motion and allows me to handle them when ready.

This technique can be beneficial when the things whirling around you are people and their emotions which can act like wrecking balls of energy. You are in control of your physical space and energy.

Grounding

Are you an electrician? I am not an electrician. And it is necessary to delve into that for just a moment. Grounding is called grounding for a reason.

A ground wire is a safety measure allowing excess electricity to be directed into the ground. If there is no outlet or way for excess electricity to escape, then it can damage the equipment or even start a fire.

Grounding is the act of focusing the excess energy from our systems (physical, mental, emotional, energetic, spiritual) and transferring that to the earth (or another source) while simultaneously bringing up energy from the earth (or another source) to heal, inspire, create, etc. The last part adds to the basic concept of electricity shared above.

Often, the image given to create a visualization for this is a tree's taproot. We are prompted to send down our taproot deep into the earth. We send down this taproot after Centering (see previous section). When we have reached the appropriate depth, we send down the excess energy we've built up. After we feel that it is moving, we are prompted to begin pulling up the healing powers from the earth to replenish us and give us sustenance. This is a good visualization technique for grounding. Visualizing and feeling may be difficult initially, but both can be strengthened and come more easily with practice.

> **Taproot** is the primary root of a primary system, growing vertically downward. Its main function is to provide a deep anchor. It aids in the absorption of nutrients and water from the soil.

By grounding your excess energy, you may decrease or eliminate the following:

- Distraction
- Anxiety
- Depression
- Restless Sleep
- Connect with the earth and receive energy
- Calmness
- Less stress on all systems
- More control over our output/words/intentions

Here are some basic steps that can be done after Centering:

1. As you continue breathing (four-fold or otherwise), feel your spine extend into the ground below you.
2. Feel the top of your spine extend up toward the sky.
3. Within the spine are two channels, one going down and one going up. Picture a full circle being made by connecting to the earth below and the sky above.
4. When you have established the flow of this cycle through you and can feel it solidly, begin to pool all the excess energy you feel in your body, mind, and spirit systems at the center of your body around the belly button.

5. When complete, release the energy into the down channel and allow it to be recycled in the earth.
6. Continue to feel the complete cycle and movement of energy through you.

This practice can also be used to help other people experiencing distress, but it has to be utilized in the right way and account for the surroundings.

You can ground into different mediums, not just Earth. Once, I was on a plane that was experiencing terrible turbulence. We flew very short distances from Salt Lake City, Utah, to Denver, Colorado. I was seated next to a friend of mine. This friend just happened to be afraid of flying and hated small spaces.

After trying to help alleviate some of their anxiety, I realized that I was experiencing them trying to ground their excess energy. Great idea! Until I realized that they were trying to ground into the earth. After my lightbulb moment, I asked them if they were grounding, and they replied yes. I wondered if they were trying to ground into the earth.

At this point, what did I have to lose? I joked that they would cause the plane to crash with the amount of power they had been trying to force to the ground. I laughed, and so did they. We switched up the tactics, and they connected to the element of air instead. It looked and worked the same as the steps described above. It worked! My friend felt better. And I'm not making this shit up; the turbulence significantly lessened.

Grounding into the four elements of Earth, Air, Fire, or Water is possible and takes some practice. We all have one that feels natural and is our most substantial ground. Once you have a feel for it with Earth, try the others. If Earth feels impossible after weeks of practice, try another one you feel more connected to.

There are many interpretations of Grounding floating around. The above is how I interpret and teach it. Earthing is another term that may be connected to Grounding. They are very different processes. Take some time to discover other ways of Centering and Grounding. Find the recipe that works for you.

Shielding

We all know what a windshield is, right? A piece of glass on your vehicle prevents you from getting bugs in your teeth and your nicely coiffed hair from being a tangled mess. It also prevents you from getting wet, dusty, and cold when the elements are less than friendly to our fragile human bodies. A personal energetic shield works similarly, except it provides a barrier that can prevent you from the intrusive and sloppy energy of other beings, including humans.

Complete the steps to Center and Ground as listed in the previous sections. When you can feel a steady flow, as listed in the last phase of Grounding, do the following:

1. Begin to separate out a little bit of the energy flowing through you and focus it into a little sphere near your belly button.
2. Focus on continuing to feed this sphere and watch it grow. The sphere will encapsulate your physical and energetic bodies.
3. Stop the growth when the sphere has expanded to approximately a foot above your head and below your feet. Allow the energy to flow through the sphere just as it does in your body: It flows from the earth into you and out to the sky, and the opposite simultaneously happens.

4. Inhale and exhale a few times.

5. On the next inhale, feel the sphere move closer to you and begin to match the shape of your body. As the sphere condenses, it becomes more robust and more impenetrable.

6. Feel the sphere settle into its new shape on the exhale.

7. Try this several times until the energy sphere has become the same shape as your body but is about six inches from your physical form's edges.

Shielding is a critical skill to develop. I need you to hear this one thing: You do not have to be available to people 24/7. It is not mean or abusive to have boundaries. It is not selfish to have boundaries. In fact, it is the best way to serve your family and community. Be sovereign. Have edges and boundaries that are healthy and keep you from being overwhelmed. You can only be productive and helpful if you are calm and focused.

This is necessary if you are also trying to develop your psychic abilities. As a reader, healer, and human being, I must distinguish my aches, pains, and emotions from those of the client I am helping. This is crucial to your success and will only be accomplished after some time. It takes time and practice.

I used to cruise through life without shields. I was blissfully wandering along, naively thinking that I was safe. I thought no one really wanted to hurt other people. I thought I was protected. I learned quickly that shields are a good practice. And although I was not harmed, I was shaken.

One day many years ago, I visited a metaphysical store, not looking for anything specific, just browsing. The month before visiting this metaphysical store, I had been doing a lot of journey work, traveling here and there astrally. The store employee, who happened to be a spirit worker, was chatting with me like a regular interaction. They then asked if I was tired. I replied yes, and that I had been busy lately. They then responded that doing so much traveling will do that to a person. Without thinking, I agreed, and then it hit me like a ton of bricks. They were reading me and "tapping in" to me. I felt violated. That was really none of their business.

This is precisely why I ask people for permission to read them before beginning. I do not believe that they had malicious intent. It just freaked me out that they could see everything. No one needs to know that much about anyone else. I only went into that place again with full shields. And on the other end of the spectrum, just a thought: If you're shielding and holding your shit together, you won't be broadcasting or spraying your energy vomit all over other people.

Wisdom for Your
Journey Onward

Man
before the separation
of
Church
Sex
&
State

Man
before the separation
of
Life
Death
&
Orgasm

Man
before the separation
of
Family
Community
&
Survival

Mann
before the separation
of
Man
Mann
&
Nature

Mann
is not meant to be
Separated

mann
Needs
mann

boundaries
are
mann's
edges
and
the seams
that hold
Mann
Together
are
sewn
from
Threads
made of
Promises
to
each
other

About The Author

Kenn was born in Salt Lake City, Utah, in 1975. He grew up in a rural town in Northern Utah, still residing in his great-grandparents' home.

Kenn has accepted the path of a Rune Walker and Shaman in the Northern Traditions of Pre-Christian Northern Europe, Norse, and Anglo-Saxon. He provides services to his local and global communities. Kenn teaches classes and provides readings, guided meditations, and healing sessions.

Remembering the Runes and growing relationships with them and the Old Gods of Northern Europe has connected Kenn to the past and his ancestors that shape his worldview. It provides him the tools to enrich his life and truly access his essence as a passionate, free being. It allows him to enjoy living life one moment at a time while respecting and admiring the cycle within which we exist.

"In this life, I strive for harmony and freedom while pursuing knowledge and experiences to enrich and enjoy my journey. I desire to take on life's experiences with ambition. I will honorably and resourcefully face the challenges placed before me."

www.ingramcontent.com/pod-product-compliance
Lightning Source LLC
Chambersburg PA
CBHW020234130626
46549CB00005B/1891